BETHANIE AND JOSH HESTERMANN

ROCKRIDGE
PRESS

Interior and Cover Designer: Richard Tapp
Art Producer: Sara Feinstein
Editor: Laura Apperson
Production Editor: Jenna Dutton
Production Manager: Jose Olivera

Photography used under license from Shutterstock.com, cover, p. 4, 7, 11-14, 16-17, 19, 23, 29, 30-31, 38, 41, 44, 61-62, 64, 67, 73-74, 81-83, 85, 91-92, 102, 117, 121, 129, 135-136, 1401-142, 146, 157, 164, 167, 172, 175- 177, 181, 183-185, 187; iStock.com, cover, p. v, vii, xi, x, viii, xi, 9, 11, 21, 23, 26-27, 29-30, 37, 60-61, 73, 75, 78-79, 84, 86, 88-89, 107, 112, 114-116, 122, 129-130, 132-134, 154-156, 202; Creative Market/Tampatra, p. 8; Science Source/Turtle Rock Scientific, p. 20; Science Source/NASA/GSFC Scientific Visualization Studio, p. 22; Science Source/DENNIS KUNKEL MICROSCOPY, p. 28; Science Source/Nature Source RF/Nancy Sefton, p. 112, Science Source/The Natural History Museum, London, p. 159; Science Source/Pacific Ring of Fire 2004 Expedition. NOAA Office of Ocean Exploration; Dr. Bob Embley, NOAA PMEL, Chief Scientist, p. 162; Science Source/National Oceanic and Atmospheric Administration, p. 169; Science Source/Jeffrey Rotman, p. 152; Library of Congress, Geography and Map Division, p. 33, 148; Library of Congress Geography and Map Division, NOAA, Photographer: Captain Albert E. Theberge, NOAA Corps (ret.), p. 33; Credit: NOAA Okeanos Explorer Program, Gulf of Mexico 2012 Expedition, p. 152; NOAA, Craig Smith, University of Hawaii, p. 163; NOAA Okeanos Explorer Program, Gulf of Mexico 2012 Expedition, p. 168; NOAA Office of Ocean Exploration and Research, Discovering the Deep: Exploring Remote Pacific MPAs, p. 169; Flickr/ TEDx Monterey, p. 35; Chip Clark/Smithsonian Institution, p. 61; Biopix: JC Schou, p. 74. All other photography used under license from Alamy.com. Author photo courtesy of Genevieve Elaine Photography.

ISBN: Print 978-1-64876-884-2
eBook 978-1-64876-885-9
R0
Printed in China

TO EMMA
AND FOREST

CONTENTS

Chapter 1: Our Awesome Ocean 1

The Blue Heart of Our Planet 2

Ocean Zones 4

Marine Drifters 6

Humans and the Ocean 8

Medicine from the Sea 10

The Big Blue 12

Salty Seas 14

All about Water 16

Sea Sounds 18

Ocean in Motion 20

Rivers in the Ocean . . . 22

One Ocean, Five Basins 24

What's a Sea? 26

Four Sensational Seas 28

Pirates, Arg! 30

Ocean Explorers 32

Marine Scientists to Know 34

Chapter 2: Go Fish 37

All about Fishes 38

Cold-Blooded Creatures 40

Fish Breath 42

Swim Like a Fish 44

THE FASCINATING OCEAN BOOK FOR KIDS

Fish Senses 46

Weird and Wacky 48

Male or Female? 50

Groups of Fishes 52

Fishes on the Move! . . . 54

The Magnificent Mola Mola 56

Spectacular Sharks . . 58

Big Sharks, Small Sharks 60

Rad Rays 62

Oh, Baby . . . Sharks and Rays 64

Notable Fishes 66

Fish Scientists 68

Chapter 3: Mammals of the sea 71

Marine Mammal Basics. 72

Simply Cetaceans 74

CONTENTS

Whale Mustaches 76

Ocean Giants. 78

The Biggest Animals on Earth 80

Don't Blow It 82

The Toothy Ones 84

Get to Know Porpoises. 86

Delightful Dolphins . . . 88

Echo . . . Echo . . . Echolocation! 90

Songs of the Sea 92

Pinnipeds 94

Seal, Sea Lion, or Fur Seal? 96

Sea Lion Fun Facts . . . 98

Seal Fun Facts 100

Walrus Fun Facts . . . 102

Manatees and Dugongs 104

Otterly Fascinating . . 106

Chapter 4: Just Coasting 109

Cool Coasts 110

Tiny Worlds 112

Interesting Invertebrates 114

Sea Jellies and Their Relatives 116

Prickly Personalities. . 118

Reef Life 120

Seahorses and Sea Dragons 122

The Great Barrier Reef 124

Reef Relationships . . 126

Cool Defenses 128

Bivalves: Better Together! 130

Kelp Forests 132

Forest Friends 134

Meadows under the Sea 136

Marine Reptiles 138

Mangroves: Trees on Stilts! 140

Exploring Estuaries . . 142

Chapter 5: Into the Deep 145

Rock Bottom 146

In the Trenches 148

The Challenger Deep 150

Deep-Sea Life 152

Tricks for Living in the Dark 154

Octopuses vs. Squids 156

Super-Sized Squids . . 158

Warmth in Cold Places 160

Deep-Sea Communities 162

Shipwrecks 164

The Unsinkable Ship . . 166

Curious Creatures of the Deep 168

Chapter 6: Pole to Pole 171

North Pole, South Pole 172

Glorious Glaciers 174

Floating Ice Mountains 176

Welcome to the Arctic 178

North Pole Residents 180

The Ultimate Pole Predator 182

Beautiful Belugas . . . 184

Unicorns of the Sea . . 186

Arctic Seabirds 188

Welcome to the Antarctic 190

Home, Chilly Home . . . 192

Seabirds of the Antarctic 194

Penguins 196

Polar Exploration . . . 198

Poles in Trouble 200

Chapter 1

OUR AWESOME OCEAN

WITHOUT THE OCEAN, LIFE COULDN'T—AND WOULDN'T—EXIST ON EARTH.

THE BLUE HEART OF OUR PLANET

There are more than **352 TRILLION GALLONS** of water in the ocean.

Water covers about 71 percent of the planet. Land covers the other 29 percent.

About 97 percent of all the water on Earth is in the ocean.

The other **3 PERCENT** of Earth's water exists as freshwater in rivers and lakes, groundwater, and ice in glaciers and ice caps.

There are more than 200,000 known animal species in the ocean, but there could be a million or more awaiting discovery.

The ocean is like a **GIANT RADIATOR.** It soaks up heat from the sun and spreads its warmth around the planet.

The ocean's **SURFACE TEMPERATURE** varies from a warm 86°F (30°C) to a frigid 28°F (-2.2°C).

OCEAN ZONES

Scientists don't know exactly, but they estimate that 90 percent of all ocean organisms live in the SUNLIGHT ZONE—mainly because there is plenty to eat there.

The top 650 feet (198 m) of ocean water is in the sunlight zone. Beneath it are the twilight, midnight, abyssal, and hadal zones. The hadal zone is everything below 3.7 miles (6 km).

Many marine animals use COUNTERSHADING for camouflage. From above, their dark back blends with deep water. From below, their light belly blends with the sunlit water.

MARINE DRIFTERS

Any aquatic organism that drifts because it can't move or is too weak to swim against the current is called **PLANKTON**.

PLANKTON includes plant-like organisms called phytoplankton and animal-like organisms called zooplankton.

Plankton is at the bottom of most marine food chains.

A single species of marine bacteria called *PROCHLOROCOCCUS* provides up to 20 percent of Earth's oxygen all by itself!

Up to 80 percent of the oxygen we breathe comes from the billions of phytoplankton in the ocean. Scientists call these phytoplankton the ocean's "invisible forest."

Every night, **ZOOPLANKTON** like krill (shrimp-like crustaceans) migrate up toward the surface of the ocean to eat phytoplankton.

PLANKTON are often tiny—less than an inch long. But sea jellies are also plankton, and they can be more than 100 feet (30 m) long.

Like land plants, **PHYTOPLANKTON** make energy from sunlight using photosynthesis.

HUMANS AND THE OCEAN

ONE IN EVERY THREE people around the world live within 60 miles (96 km) of the ocean. That's more than 2.5 billion people!

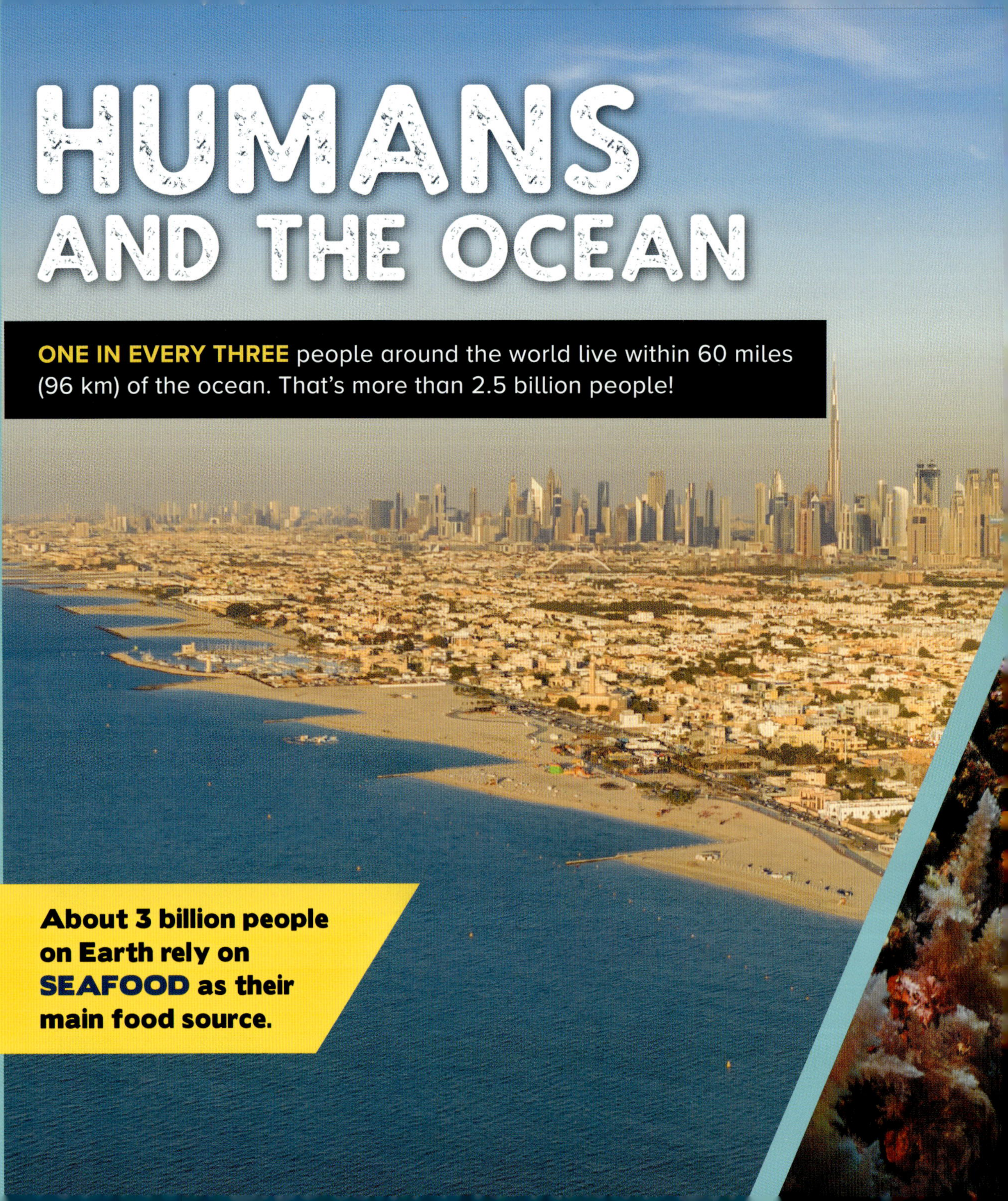

About 3 billion people on Earth rely on SEAFOOD as their main food source.

Humans put SEAWEED in products like ice cream, salad dressing, and toothpaste to thicken them up. In the ingredient list, it'll say "carrageenan"—that's seaweed!
A SCUBA diver can explore underwater for up to an hour (sometimes more!) on one tank of oxygen. SCUBA stands for "self-contained underwater breathing apparatus."

MEDICINE FROM THE SEA

Scientists study marine animals like **SPONGES** and **CORALS** to develop new medicines.

Researchers are using SEA SQUIRTS to fight cancer. Some substances in the squirts can actually shrink tumors!

CONE SNAIL VENOM can be deadly to humans, but scientists have figured out how to use it to make powerful painkillers.

A **SEA WHIP** (soft coral) from the Caribbean Sea makes chemicals that can reduce swelling and help heal wounds.

HORSESHOE CRABS have blue, copper-based blood that reacts to the presence of bacteria. Humans use it to make sure medicines, vaccines, and medical equipment are free of bacteria.

THE BIG BLUE

The ocean usually looks **BLUE** because it absorbs red light and reflects the light wavelengths humans see as blue.

Ocean water can appear green or brown, especially near coasts. Phytoplankton can make water look green, while sand or silt can make it look muddy brown.

In some cases, the ocean may look **RED**! Red tides, also called harmful algal blooms, occur when algae grow out of control.

Beach sand can be different colors, too. It can be white, black, red, and pink. There's even a beach with purple sand!

PFEIFFER BEACH in California has purplish sand because bits of manganese garnet from nearby hills have eroded onto the beach and mixed with sand grains.

SALTY SEAS

The water in the ocean is about **3.5 PERCENT SALTS.** That's too salty to drink. If you did, you'd actually get thirstier.

Vents (cracks) in the seafloor and underwater volcanic eruptions add salt to seawater.

The saltier the water, the easier it is to float in it. THE DEAD SEA is so salty, it's impossible for a person to sink!

Salt water needs to be colder than freshwater to freeze. **SALT WATER** freezes at about 28.4°F (-2°C), while freshwater freezes at 32°F (0°C).

Much of the salt in seawater comes from rocks on land. Rainwater breaks down the rocks, then streams and rivers dump the dissolved salts into the ocean.

ALL ABOUT WATER

Water can be **GAS (STEAM), LIQUID**, and **SOLID (ICE)**. Molecules are farthest apart in gases, closer in liquids, and closest together in solids.

TWO HYDROGEN ATOMS and ONE OXYGEN ATOM make up a single molecule of water.

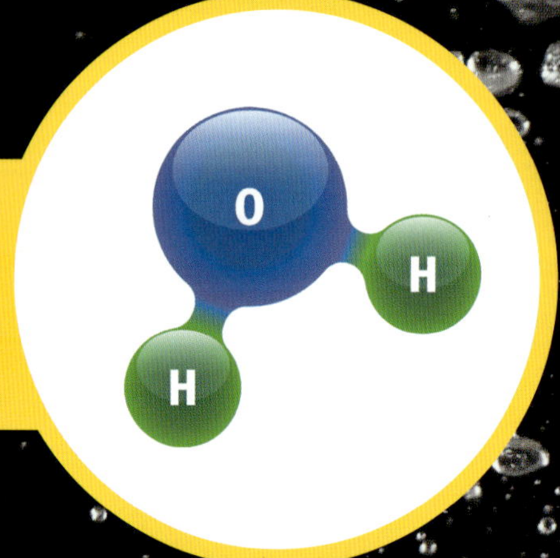

The amount of water on Earth doesn't change. The same molecules that were in the water dinosaurs drank are in the water you drink.

SEA SOUNDS

SOUND travels more than four times faster through water than through air, because molecules in liquid water are closer together than they are in air (a gas).

In the ocean, water temperature, saltiness, and depth affect how quickly sound travels. For example, sound travels faster in WARM WATER than in COLD WATER.

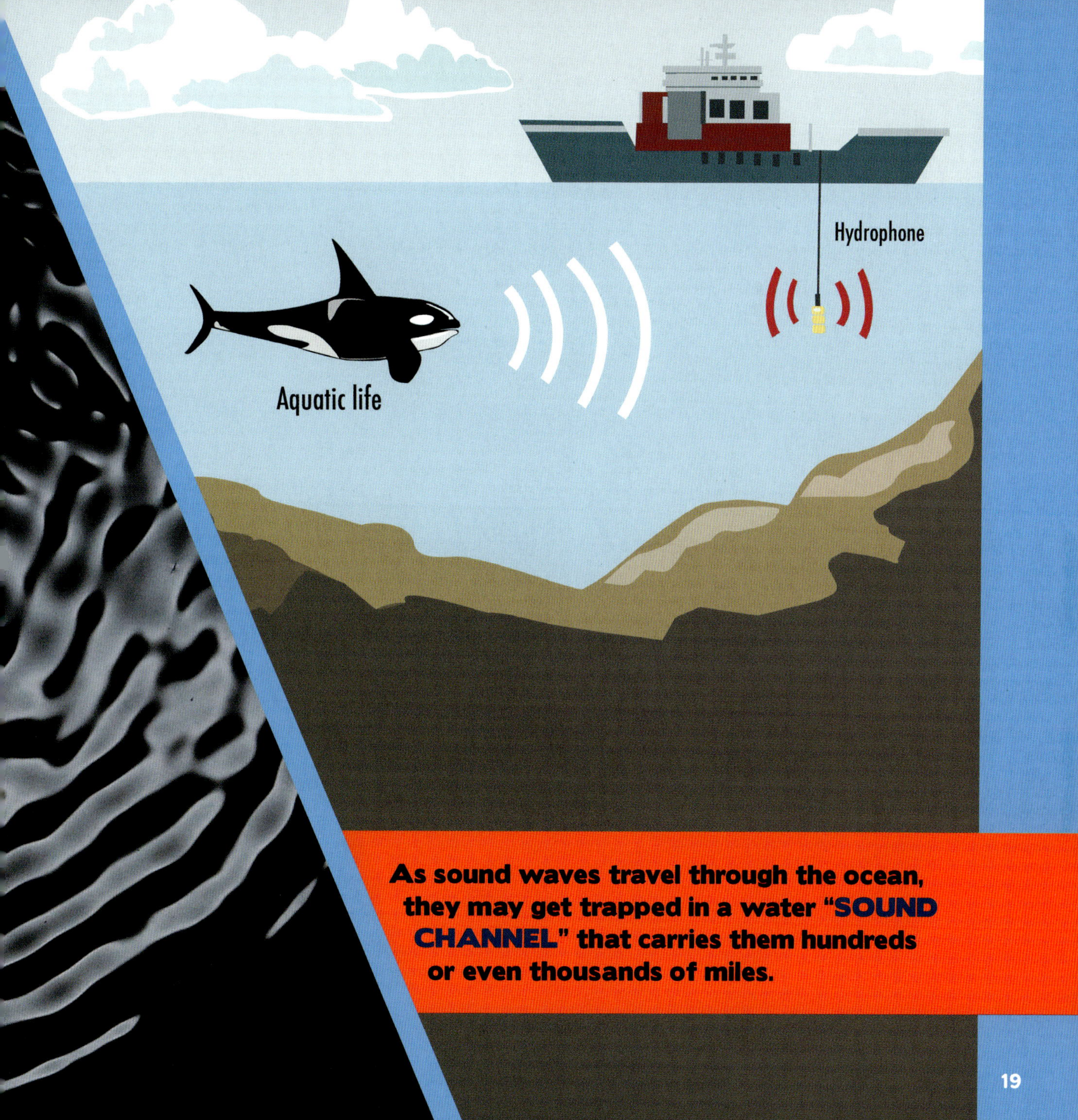

As sound waves travel through the ocean, they may get trapped in a water "**SOUND CHANNEL**" that carries them hundreds or even thousands of miles.

OCEAN IN MOTION

Wind, tides, water temperature, and saltiness all create **MOVEMENT** in the ocean.

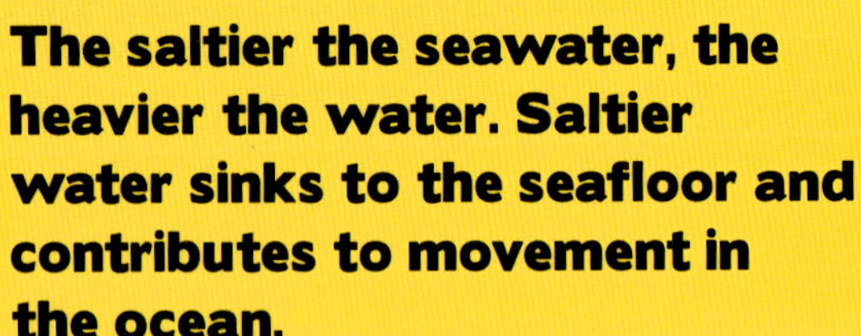

The saltier the seawater, the heavier the water. Saltier water sinks to the seafloor and contributes to movement in the ocean.

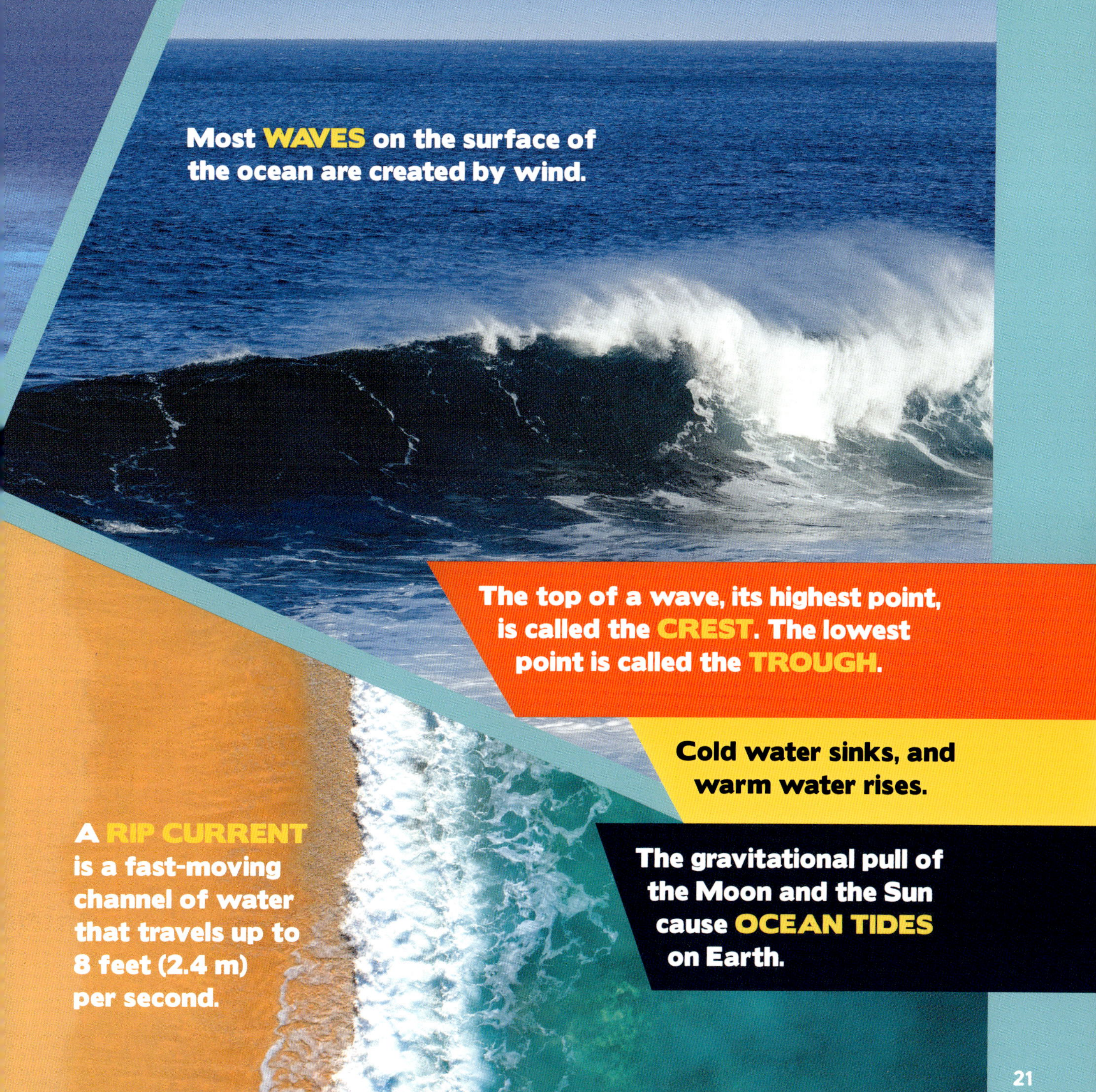

Most WAVES on the surface of the ocean are created by wind.

The top of a wave, its highest point, is called the CREST. The lowest point is called the TROUGH.

Cold water sinks, and warm water rises.

A RIP CURRENT is a fast-moving channel of water that travels up to 8 feet (2.4 m) per second.

The gravitational pull of the Moon and the Sun cause OCEAN TIDES on Earth.

RIVERS IN THE OCEAN

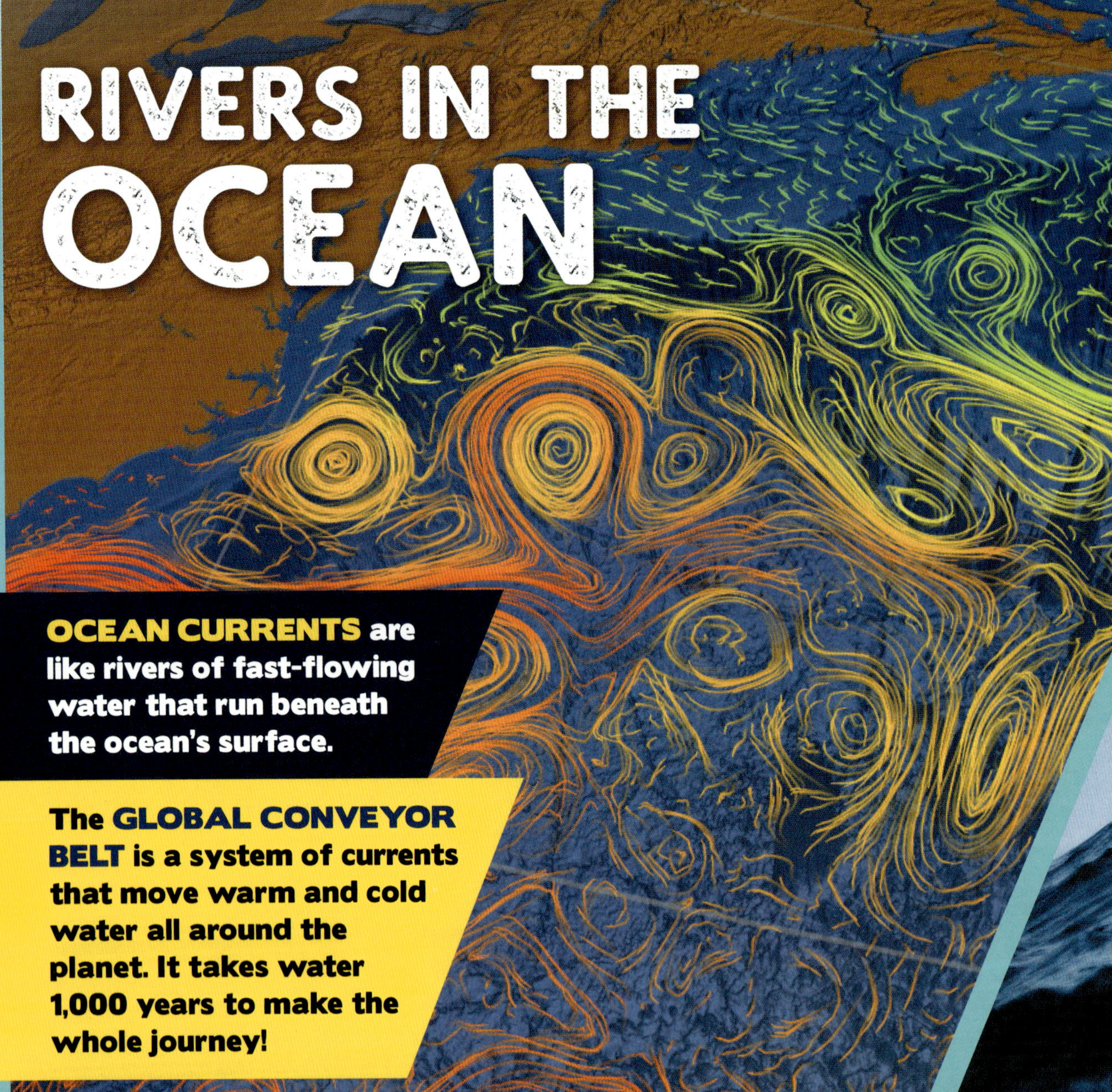

OCEAN CURRENTS are like rivers of fast-flowing water that run beneath the ocean's surface.

The **GLOBAL CONVEYOR BELT** is a system of currents that move warm and cold water all around the planet. It takes water 1,000 years to make the whole journey!

The **GULF STREAM** is a warmwater current in the Atlantic Ocean that moves nearly 4 billion cubic feet (1.29 billion cubic meters) of water per second.

The **KUROSHIO CURRENT** drives warm water across the Pacific Ocean from Japan toward North America.

In Japanese, *kuroshio* means "black current." The current earned this name because the water that flows in the current appears darker than the surrounding water.

ONE OCEAN, FIVE BASINS

There is only one **GLOBAL** ocean.

PORTUGUESE explorer Ferdinand Magellan named the Pacific in the 16th century. The word means "peaceful."

Modern scientists in the United States and many other countries divide the ocean into FIVE BASINS: Arctic, Atlantic, Indian, Pacific, and Southern.

THE PACIFIC OCEAN is the planet's largest ocean basin. All of Earth's continents could fit inside it!

THE ARCTIC OCEAN is Earth's shallowest ocean basin by far, with an average depth of less than 4,000 feet (1,219 m).

THE SOUTHERN OCEAN is also called the Antarctic Ocean, because it surrounds Antarctica.

THE ATLANTIC OCEAN or "Sea of Atlas" was named after Atlas—a figure in Greek mythology who was doomed to hold up the sky forever.

THE INDIAN OCEAN is the warmest ocean basin, with surface temperatures as high as 82°F (28°C).

WHAT'S A SEA?

A **SEA** is a body of water that's connected to the ocean but is mostly surrounded by land.

The meaning of "the Seven Seas" has changed throughout history. Different cultures have used the same phrase to refer to different sets of seven seas.

For Ancient Greeks, the "Seven Seas" were the Adriatic Sea, Aegean Sea, Black Sea, Caspian Sea, Mediterranean Sea, Red Sea, and the Persian Gulf.

FOUR SENSATIONAL SEAS

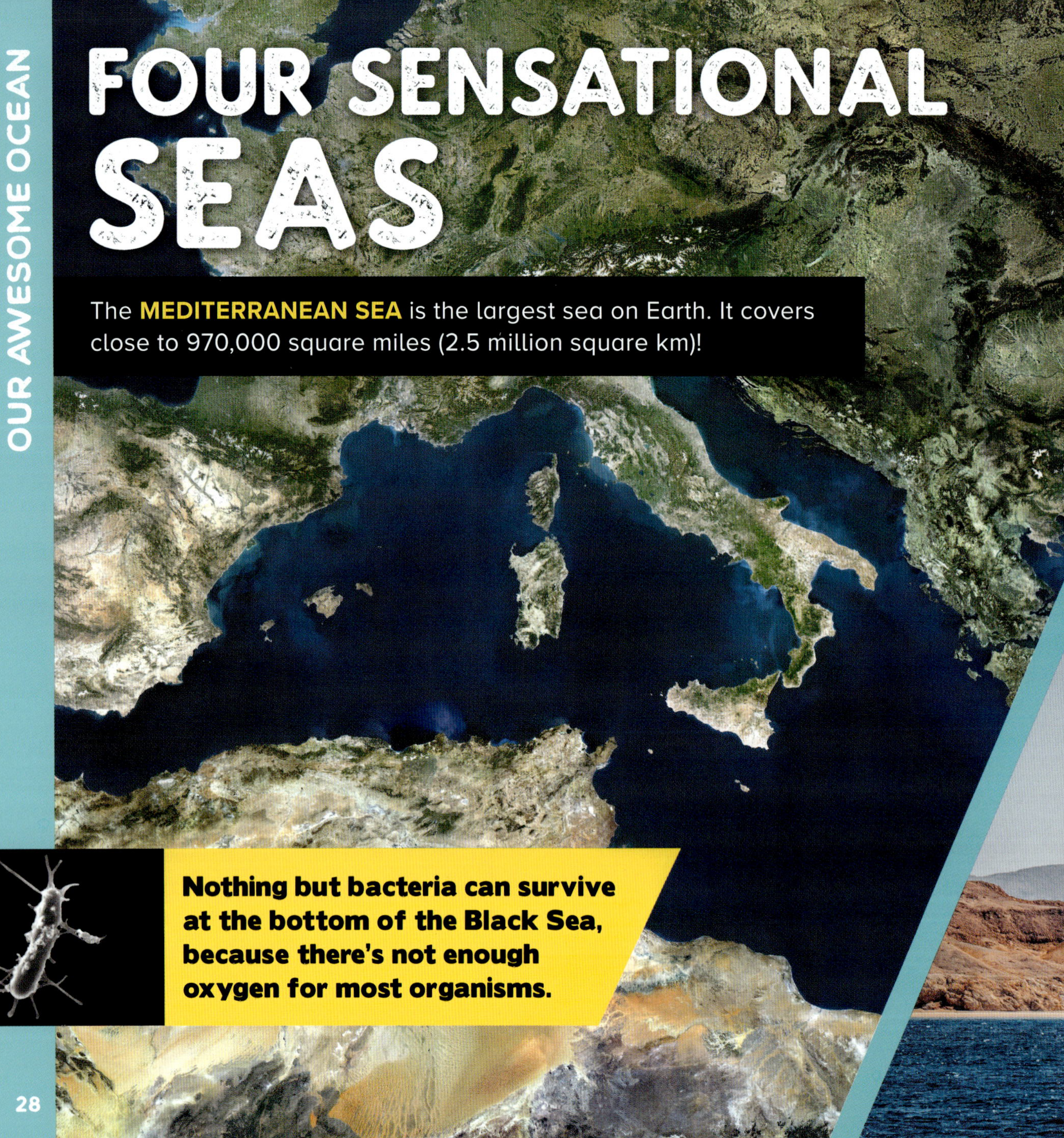

The **MEDITERRANEAN SEA** is the largest sea on Earth. It covers close to 970,000 square miles (2.5 million square km)!

Nothing but bacteria can survive at the bottom of the Black Sea, because there's not enough oxygen for most organisms.

The **ARAL SEA** is about one-tenth its original size. In the 1960s, humans began diverting the two rivers that fed the sea to irrigate crops, causing the sea to shrink.

Egypt's Red Sea is not actually red, although algae blooms sometimes make it look reddish-brown.

PIRATES, ARG!

PIRATES are robbers who plunder coastal towns and ships at sea.

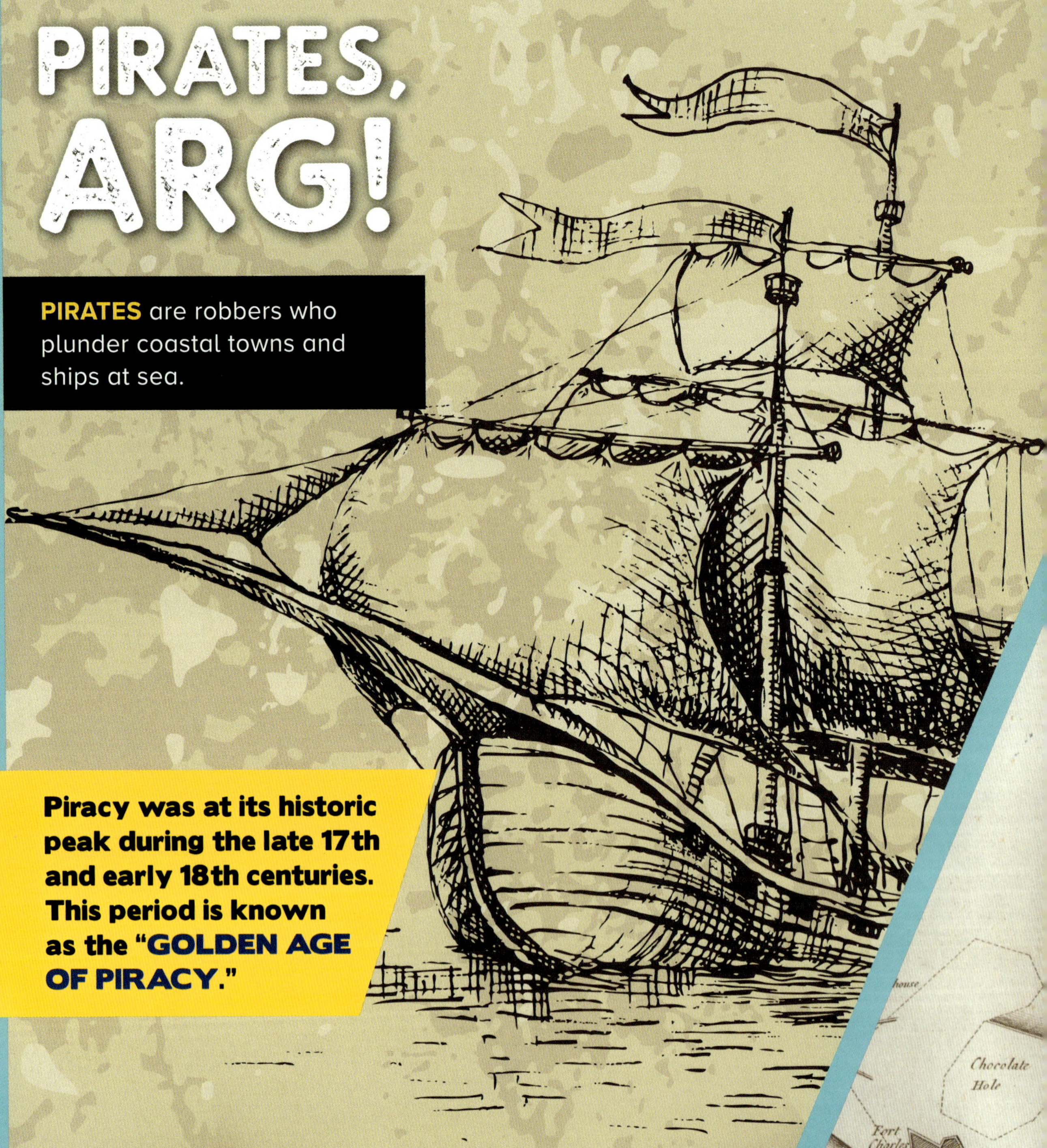

Piracy was at its historic peak during the late 17th and early 18th centuries. This period is known as the "GOLDEN AGE OF PIRACY."

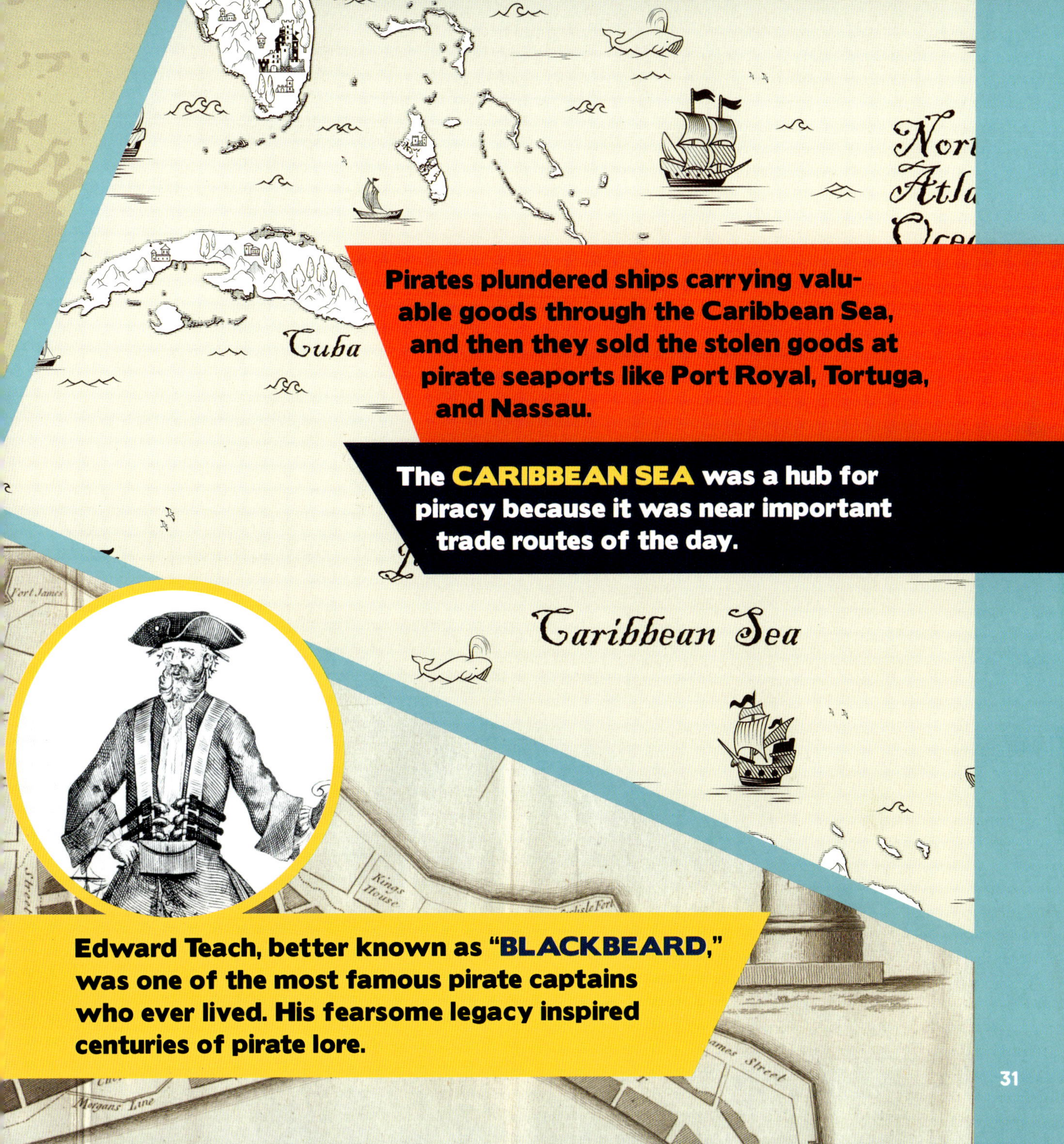

Pirates plundered ships carrying valuable goods through the Caribbean Sea, and then they sold the stolen goods at pirate seaports like Port Royal, Tortuga, and Nassau.

The CARIBBEAN SEA was a hub for piracy because it was near important trade routes of the day.

Edward Teach, better known as "BLACKBEARD," was one of the most famous pirate captains who ever lived. His fearsome legacy inspired centuries of pirate lore.

OCEAN EXPLORERS

Early Polynesian voyagers didn't have compasses, but they found their way across the Pacific Ocean using clues from the Sun, stars, and the ocean itself.

FERDINAND MAGELLAN set out on an expedition in 1519 to be the first person to sail around the world, but Magellan himself was killed on the journey.

In the 1830s, **CHARLES DARWIN** sailed around the world on the HMS *Beagle* and later proposed his theory of evolution based on what he learned.

In 1934, **WILLIAM BEEBE** and **OTIS BARTON** descended 3,000 feet (914 m) in an underwater exploration vessel called a bathysphere, which looked like a big metal ball.

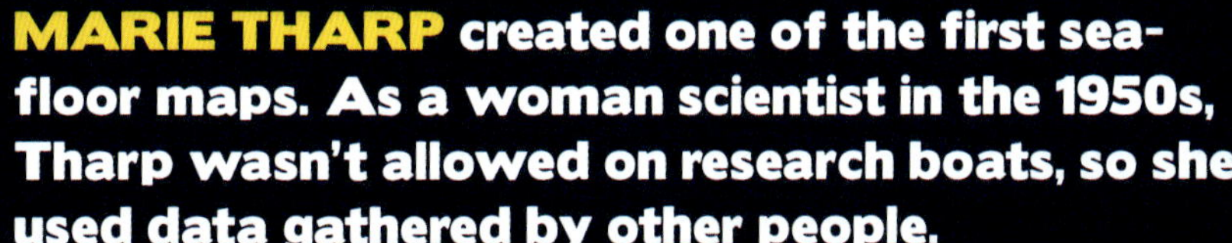

MARIE THARP created one of the first seafloor maps. As a woman scientist in the 1950s, Tharp wasn't allowed on research boats, so she used data gathered by other people.

In 1977, scientists aboard a submersible called *Alvin* discovered communities of life surrounding hot vents in the seafloor—proving life can thrive in the deep.

MARINE SCIENTISTS TO KNOW

SIR CHARLES WYVILLE THOMSON co-led the Challenger Expedition (1872–1876), which circled the globe gathering data about the ocean. It was the first expedition of its kind.

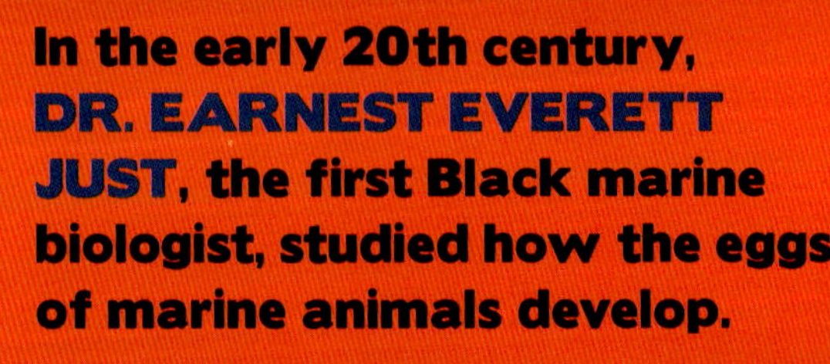

In the early 20th century, **DR. EARNEST EVERETT JUST**, the first Black marine biologist, studied how the eggs of marine animals develop.

Starting in the 1930s, **CAPTAIN JACQUES-YVES COUSTEAU** spent decades exploring what lies below the ocean's surface. He invented a small submarine called the "diving saucer" and the Aqua-Lung (used in SCUBA).

DR. SYLVIA EARLE is and has been a key marine scientist of the 20th and 21st centuries. Her research has helped scientists better understand the ocean, particularly marine algae.

DR. ASHA DE VOS is a marine biologist from Sri Lanka. She is a leading researcher and expert on blue whales, particularly those in the Indian Ocean.

Chapter 2

GO FISH

MARINE FISHES LIVE IN ALL OCEAN HABITATS—FROM THE SHALLOWEST TIDE POOLS TO THE DEEPEST TRENCHES.

ALL ABOUT FISHES

There are about 34,000 known fish species.

Fishes are VERTEBRATES, which means they have backbones (like humans and other mammals).

A freshwater fish's body concentrates salt, and a marine fish's body gets rid of extra salt. A fish that can live in freshwater and salt water can do both!

There are three major groups of fishes: bony fishes, cartilaginous fishes, and jawless fishes.

SHARKS, **RAYS**, **EELS**, and **SEAHORSES** are all fishes. These animals probably aren't what you first imagine when you think of a fish!

COLD-BLOODED CREATURES

OPAHS create heat by swimming and use that heat to warm their bodies. Researchers discovered this in 2015, making opahs the first known warm-blooded fish.

Almost all fishes are **COLD-BLOODED**. Their body temperatures are the same as the surrounding water.

A cold-blooded animal is also called an **ECTOTHERM**. *Ecto* means "outer" or "on the outside" and *therm* means "heat."

FISH BREATH

Most fish breathe using organs called **GILLS**.

A fish's gills are packed with tiny BLOOD VESSELS that collect oxygen from the water. Blood then carries the oxygen to the rest of the fish's body.

Some fish species, like **LUNGFISHES**, have lungs (or lung-like organs) *and* gills. They can breathe air if they need to!

The freshwater **AFRICAN LUNGFISH** can live outside of water, cocooned in its own mucus, for up to five years.

The **ATLANTIC TARPON** does not have lungs, but it can gulp air from the surface. The air goes into its swim bladder, which absorbs oxygen for the fish.

A fish can "drown" in water if there's not enough oxygen for it to breathe.

SWIM LIKE A FISH

Most fishes have several fins. Some, like hagfishes, have just one.

Fish fins get their names from where they are located on the fish's body: pectoral (sides), pelvic (underside), dorsal (top), and caudal (tail).

Caudal fins can be pointed, rounded, forked, or lunate (shaped like a crescent moon). The fastest fish often have lunate caudal fins.

Many fishes, including sharks, use their CAUDAL FINS to propel themselves through the water.

Some fish species, like puffers, rely on their **PECTORAL FINS** for swimming. They tend to move more slowly than species that use their caudal fins to swim.

Some fish species, including trigger-fishes, can swim **BACKWARD**.

SEAHORSES swim upright and use their dorsal fins for propulsion.

An organ called a **SWIM BLADDER** helps some fishes stay buoyant. The bladder inflates to help the fish float and deflates to help it sink.

FISH SENSES

In addition to their senses of smell, taste, hearing, and sight, fishes can also sense electric currents. This sense is called **ELECTRORECEPTION**.

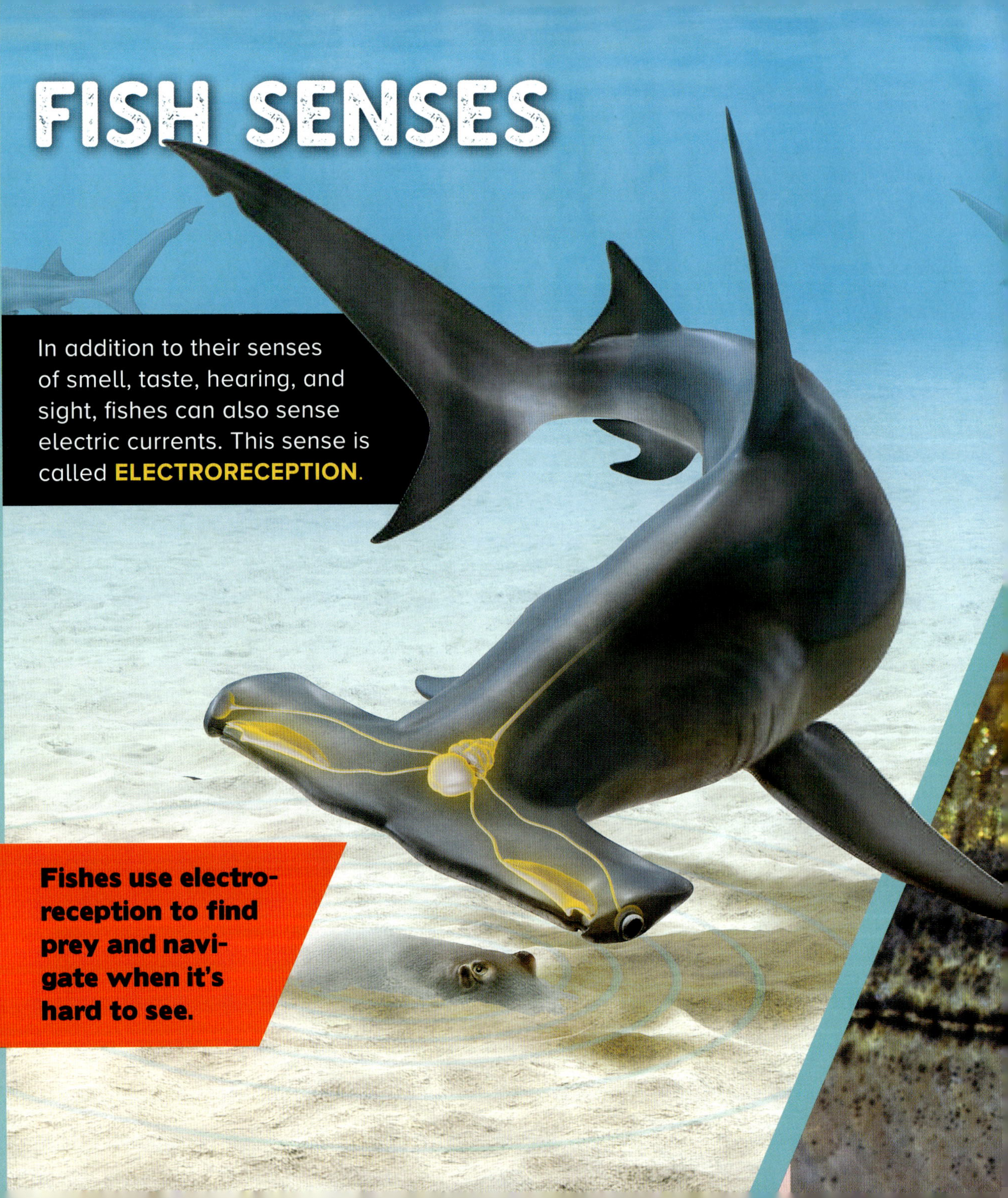

Fishes use electroreception to find prey and navigate when it's hard to see.

Not all fishes rely on their sense of sight. In fact, the blind Mexican cavefish doesn't even *have* eyes.

CATFISHES have tastebuds all over their bodies—including their whisker-like barbels. They use this extraordinary sense of taste to find food in muddy places.

A fish's **LATERAL LINE** is a system of special organs that sense vibration and pressure changes in the water.

WEIRD AND WACKY

WHITE GRUNT FISH can make a grunting noise by grinding their teeth.

FLATFISHES like halibut aren't born flat. As they grow, they flatten out—and one eye migrates to join the other one, so both eyes end up on the same side.

PARROTFISHES poop white sand.

Hawaii's state fish is the humuhumunukunukuapua'a—also called the **REEF TRIGGERFISH**. Its name means "trigger fish with a snout like a pig."

FLYING FISHES "take off" by swimming toward the surface at about 35 miles (56 km) per hour. After they break the surface, they can glide through the air for about 650 feet (198 m)!

Certain **CATFISHES** swim upside down . . . on purpose! This helps the fish feed at the surface of the water and breathe air when oxygen is low.

A **MANGROVE RIVULUS** will eat another mangrove rivulus's eggs, but it won't eat its own eggs.

If they have enough space and food, many fish species will keep growing throughout their entire lives!

MALE OR FEMALE?

Many fishes are sequential **HERMAPHRODITES**. In other words, they can switch genders at some point in their lives.

While most fishes can only change gender in one direction, BLUE-BANDED GOBIES can change genders in both directions—multiple times!

Female BLUEHEAD WRASSES can change from female to male in about 20 days.

It's common for sequential hermaphrodites to change from female to male, but pretty rare for them to change from male to female.

A social group of **CLOWNFISH** includes just one female. When she dies, the largest, most dominant male fish in the group becomes female to take her place.

The **DWARF HAWKFISH** can change from female to male and then back to female if challenged by a more powerful male.

GROUPS OF FISHES

SHOALING is different from schooling. A shoal is a group of fish living together but moving independently.

When a group of fish swims together in a coordinated way, it's called **SCHOOLING**.

A SCHOOL OF HERRING could contain millions of individuals!

FISHES ON THE MOVE!

Many fishes **MIGRATE** (travel from one place to another at the same time each year). Every year, North Pacific albacore tuna travel back and forth across the Pacific Ocean between Japan and the United States.

Some fish species, including ATLANTIC SALMON, are born in freshwater, move to the ocean, then migrate back to freshwater to spawn.

Other species, including the **NORTH AMERICAN EEL**, do the reverse. They're born in the ocean, move to freshwater, then migrate back to the ocean to breed.

Most fishes **LAY EGGS**. Many species spawn, releasing thousands or even millions of eggs at once!

THE MAGNIFICENT MOLA MOLA

FEMALE MOLA MOLAS can release 300 million eggs at a time—more than any other known vertebrate on Earth.

Mola molas can be almost 11 feet (3.3 m) long and weigh 4,000 or more pounds (1,814 kg). That's as heavy as a car!

The mola mola has several nicknames. These include "**OCEAN SUNFISH**" and "**SWIMMING HEAD**," because the fish looks like it's all head and no body.

The **MOLA MOLA** spends a lot of time sunning itself. It does this by floating horizontally at the water's surface.

A mola mola's teeth are fused together, kind of like a **BIRD'S BEAK**.

SPECTACULAR SHARKS

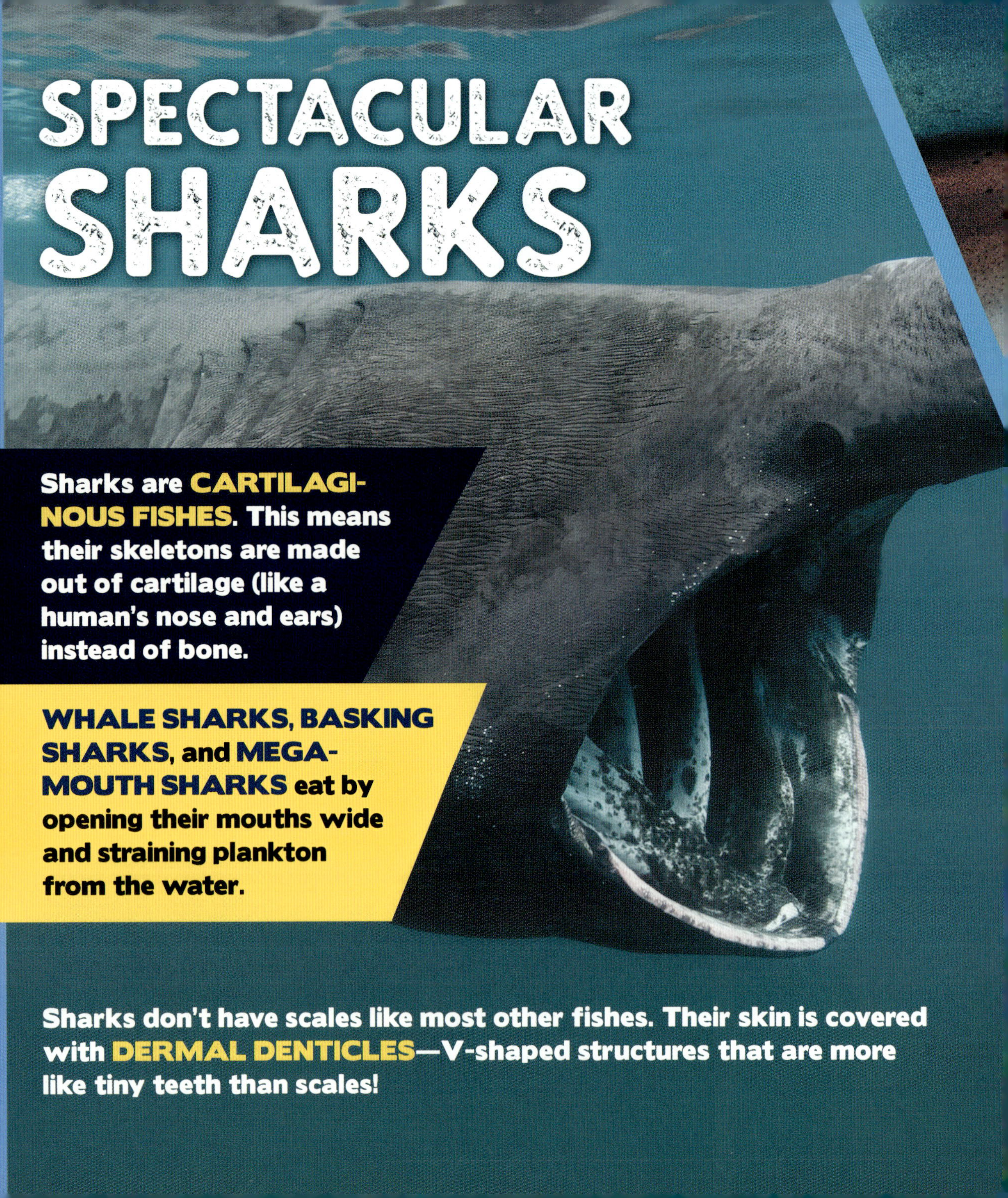

Sharks are **CARTILAGINOUS FISHES**. This means their skeletons are made out of cartilage (like a human's nose and ears) instead of bone.

WHALE SHARKS, BASKING SHARKS, and **MEGAMOUTH SHARKS** eat by opening their mouths wide and straining plankton from the water.

Sharks don't have scales like most other fishes. Their skin is covered with **DERMAL DENTICLES**—V-shaped structures that are more like tiny teeth than scales!

Unlike most fishes, sharks have **EYELIDS**.

Sharks don't hunt humans. In fact, lightning kills more people each year than sharks.

Sharks have up to 50 **ROWS OF TEETH**. When one tooth falls out, a new one moves forward to replace it.

Some sharks hunt large prey, like seals and sea lions, while others eat tiny plankton.

Dermal denticles make a shark's skin feel smooth one way (from head to tail) and like sandpaper the other way (from tail to head).

BIG SHARKS, SMALL SHARKS

The largest fish in the ocean is the **GIGANTIC WHALE SHARK**. It can be more than 40 feet (12 m) long—about as long as a school bus.

Not all sharks are big. About half of all shark species measure 3 feet (0.9 m) or less.

A full-grown **DWARF LANTERNSHARK** can fit in the palm of a human hand.

Long extinct, the **MEGALODON SHARK** was about 60 feet (18 m) long. It had a 10-foot-wide (3 m) mouth and teeth up to 7 inches (17 cm) long—the length of a banana!

RAD RAYS

RAYS are cartilaginous fishes and have flexible cartilage skeletons, just like sharks.

Many rays have fused teeth called **CRUSHING PLATES** that are strong enough to crunch the hard shells of their prey.

STINGRAYS are a group of rays that have barbs near their long whiplike tails. These barbs inject a harmful substance called venom into their attackers.

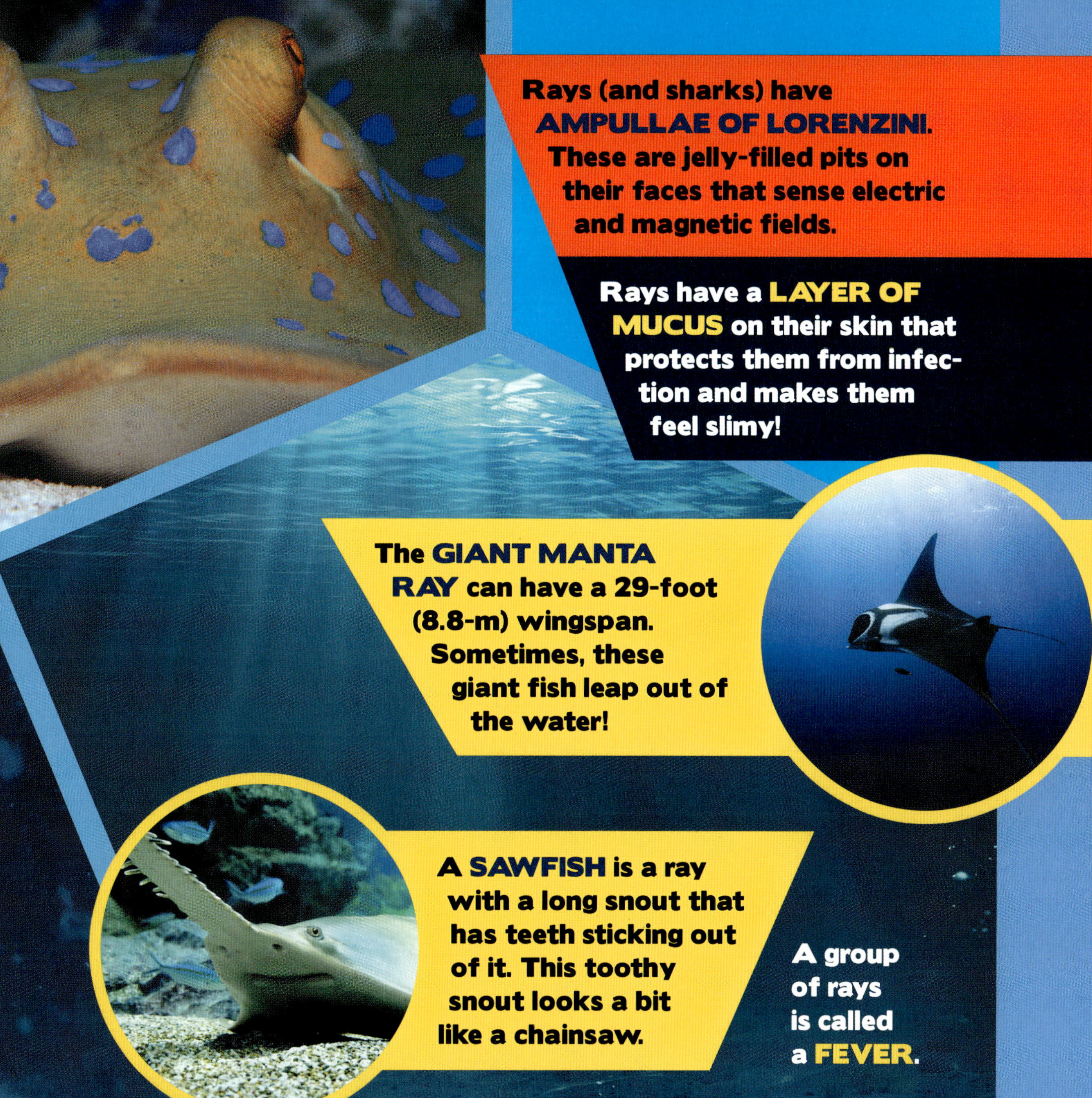

Rays (and sharks) have **AMPULLAE OF LORENZINI**. These are jelly-filled pits on their faces that sense electric and magnetic fields.

Rays have a **LAYER OF MUCUS** on their skin that protects them from infection and makes them feel slimy!

The **GIANT MANTA RAY** can have a 29-foot (8.8-m) wingspan. Sometimes, these giant fish leap out of the water!

A **SAWFISH** is a ray with a long snout that has teeth sticking out of it. This toothy snout looks a bit like a chainsaw.

A group of rays is called a **FEVER**.

OH, BABY . . . SHARKS AND RAYS

Some sharks lay eggs, and some—including hammerheads and great whites—give birth to **LIVE YOUNG**.

SKATES (a type of ray) lay eggs in black, rectangular cases. A shark or ray egg case is also called a mermaid's purse.

Shark and ray babies are called PUPS.

Port Jackson sharks lay eggs in **SPIRAL EGG CASES** that look like corkscrews.

NOTABLE FISHES

One of the smallest known vertebrates in the world is the **STOUT INFANTFISH**. It is about a quarter of an inch (7 mm) long—which is about the width of a pencil!

GREENLAND SHARKS have the longest known lifespan of any vertebrate on Earth. The oldest ones have lived for close to 400 years!

The coral reef **PYGMY GOBY** has the shortest known lifespan of any vertebrate—just eight weeks.

Many consider the **SAILFISH** to be the fastest fish in the ocean. It can swim about 70 miles (112 km) per hour—as fast as a car driving at highway speeds.

FISH SCIENTISTS

A person who studies fishes is called an "**ICHTHYOLOGIST**."

DR. EUGENIE CLARK was a pioneer ichthyologist whose work with sharks earned her the nickname "the Shark Lady."

Ichthyologist **DR. JOHN RANDALL** named more than 800 species during his long career studying reef fishes.

Chapter 3

MAMMALS OF THE SEA

MARINE MAMMALS INCLUDE CETACEANS (WHALES, DOLPHINS, AND PORPOISES), PINNIPEDS (SEALS, SEA LIONS, AND WALRUSES), SIRENIANS (MANATEES AND DUGONGS), AND MARINE FISSIPEDS (POLAR BEARS AND SEA OTTERS).

MARINE MAMMAL BASICS

Mammals are **ENDOTHERMIC**, or "warm-blooded." Their bodies can produce heat and maintain a stable body temperature.

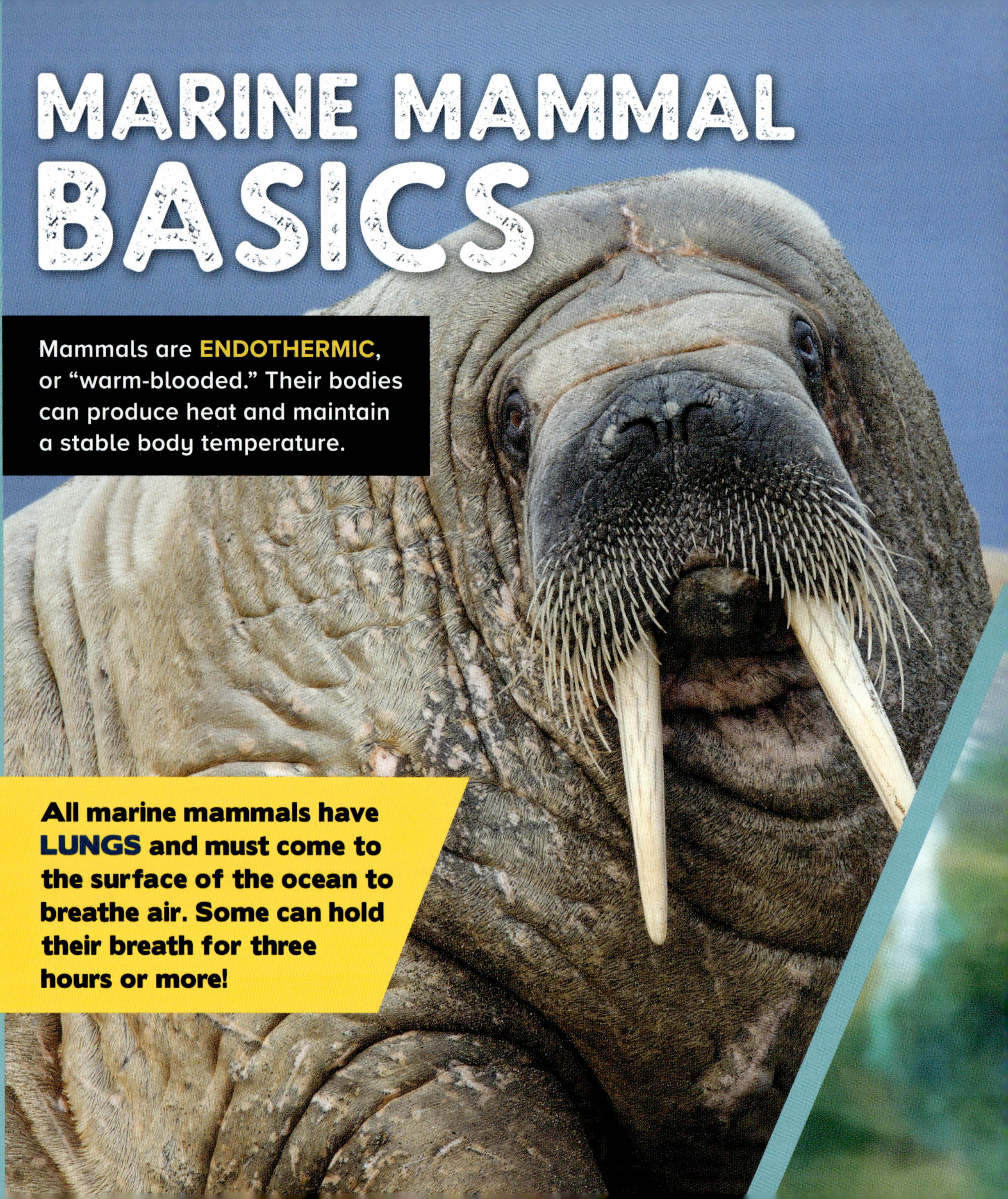

All marine mammals have LUNGS and must come to the surface of the ocean to breathe air. Some can hold their breath for three hours or more!

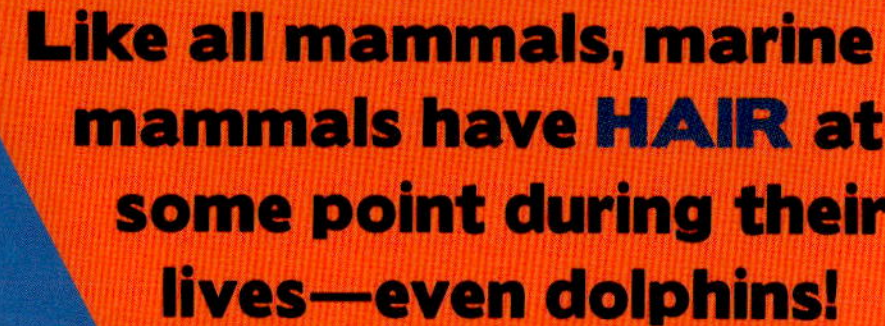

Like all mammals, marine mammals have HAIR at some point during their lives—even dolphins!

BABY DOLPHINS have little hairs on their faces when they're born, but these whisker-like hairs soon fall out.

Marine mammals give birth to live young, and female marine mammals nurse their babies after they're born.

Many marine mammals have a layer of fat called BLUBBER to help keep them warm in the water.

SIMPLY CETACEANS

There are two major groups of cetaceans: **BALEEN WHALES** and **TOOTHED WHALES**.

Dolphins have cone-shaped teeth, while their porpoise cousins have spade-shaped teeth.

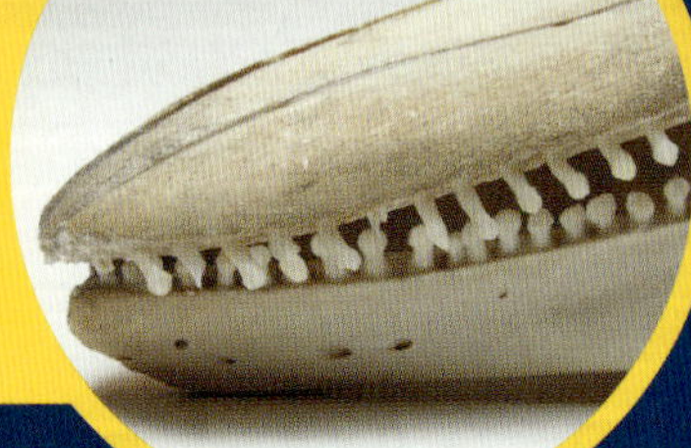

DOLPHINS are a group of toothed whales. This means all dolphins are whales . . . but not all whales are dolphins.

Toothed whales can't smell, but baleen whales can. Scientists believe baleen whales may use their sense of smell to find krill to eat.

BALEEN WHALES tend to be bigger than their toothed relatives and include the larg-est animals in the world.

WHALE MUSTACHES

Baleen whales are also called "**MYSTICETES**." The name comes from the Greek word for mustache.

A whale's "mustache" is actually bristly baleen. BALEEN are plates in the whale's mouth that are made of keratin, just like your hair and fingernails.

A bowhead whale's baleen can be 13 feet (4 m) long.

Baleen whales don't have teeth. They use baleen to strain plankton from water (the same way a pasta strainer drains the water and leaves the pasta).

Baleen is also called "**WHALEBONE**" (even though it's not bone!). People once used baleen to make things like corsets and umbrella ribs.

OCEAN GIANTS

Bowhead whales, right whales, blue whales, minke whales, fin whales, humpback whales, and gray whales are all baleen whales.

Some baleen whales, like right whales, are SKIMMERS. They feed by swimming through a swarm of plankton with their mouths wide open.

"**GULPERS**," like blue whales and humpback whales, feed by swallowing huge amounts of water, then pushing the water out through their baleen, trapping plankton inside.

Whales that feed by gulping have **THROAT GROOVES** that expand when feeding. Fin whales can gulp more than 18,000 gallons (68,000 liters) of water at once!

Gray whales don't skim or gulp. They slurp their food off the seafloor.

Gray whales migrate farther than any other mammal—about 10,000 miles (16,090 km) round trip.

THE BIGGEST ANIMALS ON EARTH

Blue whales are the **LARGEST ANIMALS THAT HAVE EVER LIVED ON EARTH**. They can be 100 feet (30 m) long and weigh 400,000 pounds (181,400 kg)!

Blue whales' bellies sometimes have a yellowish tint from the algae living on their skin.

A blue whale's TONGUE can weigh as much as an elephant.

Blue whale babies (called **CALVES**) are about 25 feet (7.6 m) long at birth!

A BLUE WHALE CALF nurses for the first 6 to 8 months of its life. It gains up to 200 pounds (90 kg) a day. That's about as heavy as a human man.

DON'T BLOW IT

A cetacean breathes through a **BLOWHOLE**—basically a nostril on top of its head.

Baleen whales have two blowholes, and toothed whales have just one.

When a cetacean surfaces to take a breath, it lets out a big, misty exhale called a "BLOW."

A blow can be 20 feet (6.1 m) high!

RIGHT WHALES have a distinct V-shaped blow.

Whale watchers can identify species by observing the shape and height of a whale's blow.

THE TOOTHY ONES

Sperm whales, beaked whales, dolphins, and porpoises are all **TOOTHED WHALES**, which are also called "odontocetes" from the Greek word for teeth.

Toothed whales are ACTIVE PREDATORS that eat fishes, squids, octopuses, and, in some cases, other marine mammals.

The SPERM WHALE is the largest of the toothed whales. It has a large rectangular-shaped head that takes up one-third of its total body length.

Scientists know fairly little about **BEAKED WHALES**. Researchers discovered a new beaked whale species (*Berardius minimus*) off the coast of Japan in 2019.

A **SPERM WHALE** has an organ filled with up to 530 gallons (2,006 liters) of fluid in its head. This organ probably helps sperm whales dive very deep to hunt.

Cuvier's beaked whales are deep-divers that can stay underwater for more than three hours. The longest recorded dive was 3 hours and 42 minutes!

GET TO KNOW PORPOISES

There are only seven **PORPOISE** species in the world. Though they look like dolphins, they are their own group.

The tiny 5-foot-long (1.5 m) VAQUITA is the smallest cetacean. These porpoises are nearly extinct because they get caught in fishermen's gillnets in Mexico's Gulf of California.

The super-speedy DALL'S PORPOISE can swim up to 34 miles (55 km) per hour, making it the fastest known porpoise on Earth.

HARBOR PORPOISES eat almost constantly. They hunt up to 550 small fishes every hour and successfully capture 90 percent of their prey.

DELIGHTFUL DOLPHINS

About 40 **DOLPHIN SPECIES** live on Earth. This includes a few species that live in freshwater, like the pink Amazon river dolphin.

When a dolphin sleeps, it shuts off half of its brain at a time. After about two hours, the dolphin switches and rests the other side.

Dolphins don't drink water because they get all the water they need from the food they eat.

DOLPHINS are social, playful, and intelligent. They can learn new skills and solve problems, sometimes by working together.

ORCAS (also called killer whales) and **PILOT WHALES** are actually dolphins. Orcas are the largest dolphins on Earth, and pilot whales are the second largest.

Orcas are top ocean predators. Some eat marine mammals like seals, sea lions, and even minke whales. Others eat fishes, particularly salmon.

ECHO . . . ECHO . . . ECHOLOCATION!

Toothed whales use **ECHOLOCATION** to find prey, navigate underwater, and communicate with each other.

To echolocate, toothed whales produce a SERIES OF CLICKS and listen for the sound waves that travel back to them after bouncing off objects.

There's a special organ in toothed whales' foreheads called a **MELON**. It helps focus the sound used in echolocation.

SONGS OF THE SEA

BOTTLENOSE DOLPHINS have a signature whistle that's special to each individual—kind of like a name.

BALEEN WHALES communicate with each other using very low, very loud sounds that travel across entire ocean basins.

MALE HUMPBACKS within the same population sing the same song—perhaps to attract mates. The song changes little by little every year.

Humpbacks "sing" by stringing many different sounds together in a pattern, just like a song. They can even use parts of songs they've learned from other whales!

PINNIPEDS

Seals, sea lions, and walruses are all **PINNIPEDS**. The word pinniped means "fin-footed."

All 33 species of pinniped are **CARNIVOROUS PREDATORS**, which means they hunt other animals for food.

These **FIN-FOOTED MARINE MAMMALS** live part of the time in the water and partly on land.

All pinnipeds have **SENSITIVE WHISKERS** that help them find food.

SEAL, SEA LION, OR FUR SEAL?

Seals and sea lions may look similar, but they are different animals. There are several ways to tell them apart.

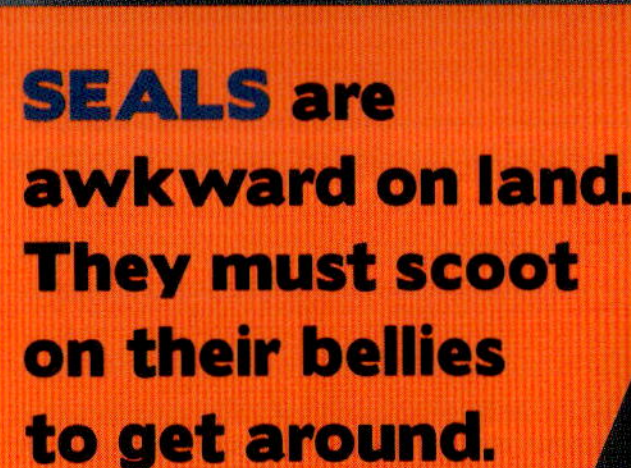

SEALS are awkward on land. They must scoot on their bellies to get around.

SEA LIONS have long front flippers and can rotate their back flippers to help them move on land. Their run looks like a gallop!

Sea lions have **EAR FLAPS**, while seals don't.

Fur seals are more like sea lions than seals. Unlike sea lions, however, fur seals have a bonus layer of thick hair called **UNDERFUR**.

SEA LION FUN FACTS

Male sea lions are much larger than females. Males of some species also grow a **MANE** around their necks, like male lions.

Sea lions can have dark brown or black teeth. Over time, healthy bacteria make a sea lion's white teeth turn partially or completely dark.

Sea lions are playful, social, and noisy. They live in large groups called **COLONIES**.

Sea lions can **COLLAPSE THEIR LUNGS** to help them dive deeper—sometimes as deep as 900 feet (274 m).

SEAL FUN FACTS

Seals can sleep underwater. Some sleep while floating vertically with just their snouts above the water. This is called "**BOTTLING**."

Male elephant seals are massive. They can be 21 feet (6.4 m) long and weigh more than 7,000 pounds (3,200 kg).

ELEPHANT SEALS get their name from the males' trunk-like snouts. Males inflate their snouts and fight each other to claim territory during breeding season.

Most seals eat fishes, shellfishes, and crustaceans, but some—like leopard seals—eat penguins and even other seals.

WALRUS FUN FACTS

WALRUS SKIN can be up to 2 inches (5 cm) thick, and their large, blubbery bodies are covered by short hairs.

Both male and female walruses have TUSKS. These long teeth never stop growing and can be up to 3 feet (1 m) long—about the height of a 3-year-old human!

Walruses use their **WHISKERY MUSTACHES** to feel around the seafloor for shellfishes.

The walrus's scientific name—*Odobenus rosmarus*—means "**TOOTH WALKING SEA HORSE.**"

MANATEES AND DUGONGS

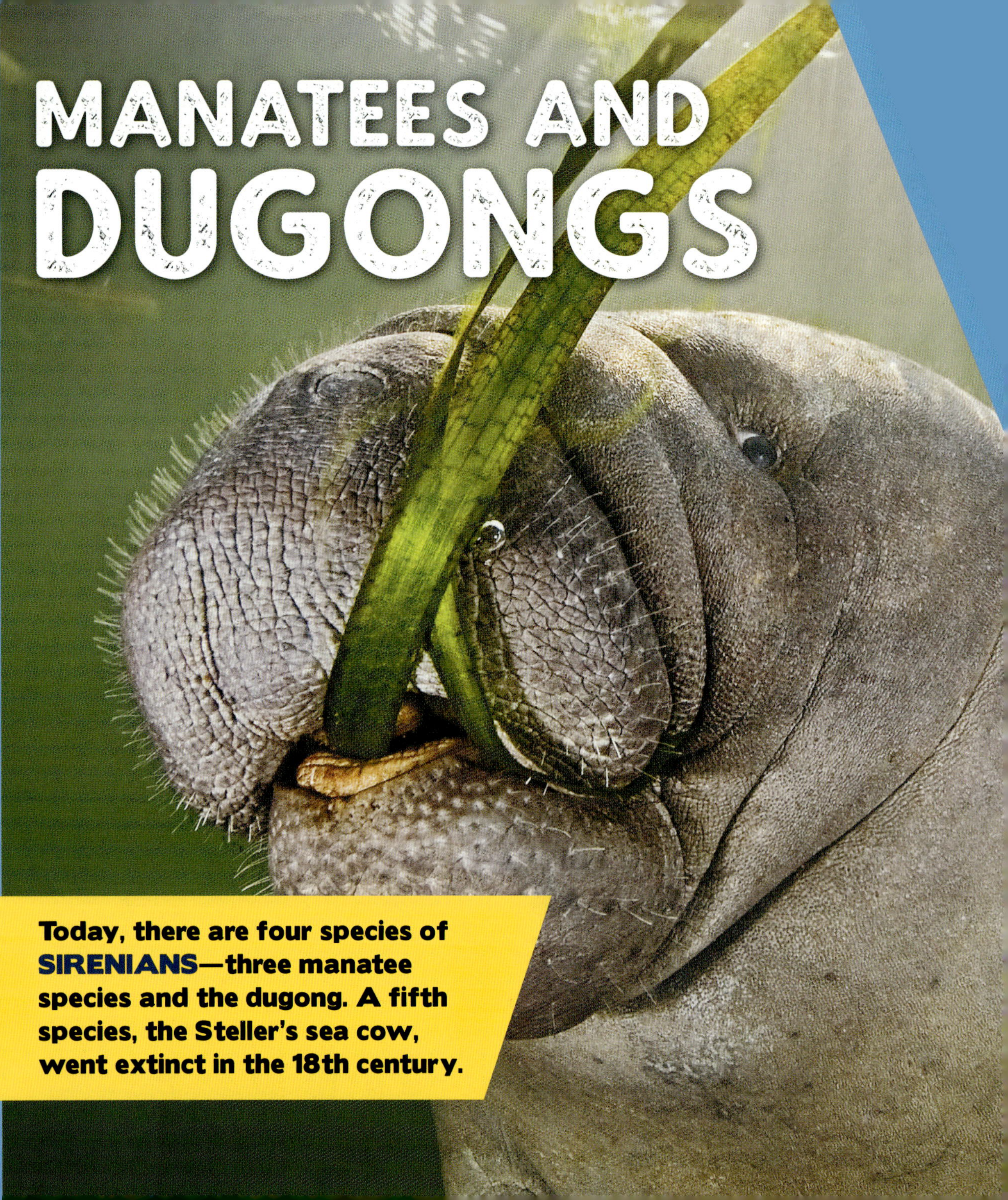

Today, there are four species of SIRENIANS—three manatee species and the dugong. A fifth species, the Steller's sea cow, went extinct in the 18th century.

West Indian and West African manatees have **TOENAILS** on their flippers, but Amazonian manatees do not.

Manatees have paddle-shaped tails, and dugongs have fluked tails.

ELEPHANTS are manatees' and dugongs' closest living relatives in the animal kingdom.

MANATEES and **DUGONGS** are the only herbivorous (plant-eating) marine mammals. They live in shallow water near coasts and eat seagrasses.

Sailors throughout history may have mistaken manatees and dugongs for **MERMAIDS**.

OTTERLY FASCINATING

Sea otters have the **DENSEST FUR** of any animal—1 million or more hairs per square inch (165,000 per square cm). Sea otters rely on their dense fur coat to keep warm, since they don't have blubber.

Sea otters link their arms while they sleep to keep from floating away from the group. This is called "RAFTING."

Sea otters nearly went EXTINCT. Humans used to hunt them for their fur during the 18th and 19th centuries.

A SEA OTTER spends up to half the day foraging and eats about 25 percent of its body weight in food every single day.

A sea otter uses its **POCKETS**—flaps of loose skin under each armpit—to store extra bits of food or even its favorite rock.

Sea otters sometimes have **PURPLE BONES**! Pigment from the spines of purple sea urchins (a favorite food) can actually stain the otters' teeth and bones.

Chapter 4

JUST COASTING

COASTAL ECOSYSTEMS ARE WIDELY STUDIED, BUT SCIENTISTS STILL DON'T KNOW HOW MANY ANIMAL SPECIES LIVE NEAR COASTS. THERE COULD BE MILLIONS!

COOL COASTS

A **COASTLINE** is always changing. Waves, wind, ocean tides, and ocean currents all help form a coast.

In 2014, an UNDERWATER VOLCANO erupted in the South Pacific Ocean, forming one of Earth's newest coastlines—an entirely new island called Hunga Tonga-Hunga Ha'apai.

COASTAL ECOSYSTEMS include tide pools, coral reefs, kelp forests, seagrass meadows, estuaries, and mangroves.

COASTAL UPWELLING pulls cold, nutrient-rich water up toward the surface near coasts. This water is perfect for supporting a diverse community of marine life.

TINY WORLDS

A **TIDE POOL** forms when the tide goes out and leaves a pool of seawater on the beach or among rocks.

Anemones, sea stars, sea snails, sea urchins, shrimps, small fishes, and even octopuses are some of the animals that may live in a tide pool.

TIDE POOL FISHES—like the tidepool sculpin, opaleye, and monkeyface eel—can breathe air if oxygen levels in the tide pool water get too low.

The **ROCK GOBY** uses camouflage to hide in its tide pool habitat. This fish can change colors in less than a minute to better match its background.

Tide pool animals must be able to handle wind and waves. Some, like **BARNACLES**, cement themselves to rocks to keep from floating away.

SEA SNAILS CALLED LIMPETS have a suction-cup foot on their undersides. Their bodies ooze a slime that acts like strong glue to help them cling to rocks.

Most tide pool animals are **INVERTEBRATES**—animals without backbones.

INTERESTING INVERTEBRATES

There are millions of **INVERTEBRATES** in the ocean, including sponges, corals, anemones, sea jellies, sea stars, sea urchins, crabs, shrimps, sea slugs, octopuses, and squids!

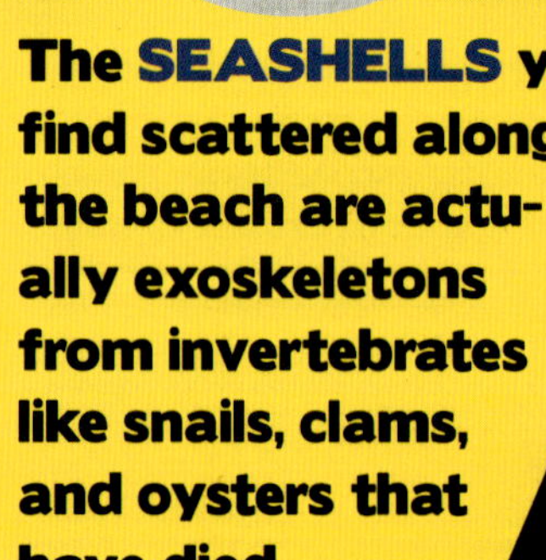

The SEASHELLS you find scattered along the beach are actually exoskeletons from invertebrates like snails, clams, and oysters that have died.

Many invertebrates, including crabs, lobsters, clams, and barnacles, have a hard casing that protects their soft bodies. This is called an EXOSKELETON.

Invertebrates can be so tiny you need a microscope to see them, like some zooplankton, or they can be huge, like the giant squid.

Some invertebrates, including crabs, lobsters, shrimps, krill, and other crustaceans, must shed their exoskeletons and build new ones as they grow.

When crustaceans that live in polluted water shed their exoskeletons, they shed toxic metals like lead from their bodies as well.

HERMIT CRABS are invertebrates that live in other animals' empty shells. They can't grow their own and need something to protect their soft bodies.

SEA JELLIES AND THEIR RELATIVES

Since jellies aren't fish, scientists call these invertebrates **SEA JELLIES** instead of jellyfish.

Sea jellies don't have bones, blood, hearts, or brains. Their bodies are 95 percent water.

Many jellies have STINGING TENTACLES that hang from a bell-shaped body. A jelly uses its tentacles to sting and stun prey like zooplankton and to bring food to its mouth.

Upside-down jellies rest upside down on the shallow seafloor to expose their bodies to sunlight. Algae living in the jellies' tissues need sunlight for energy.

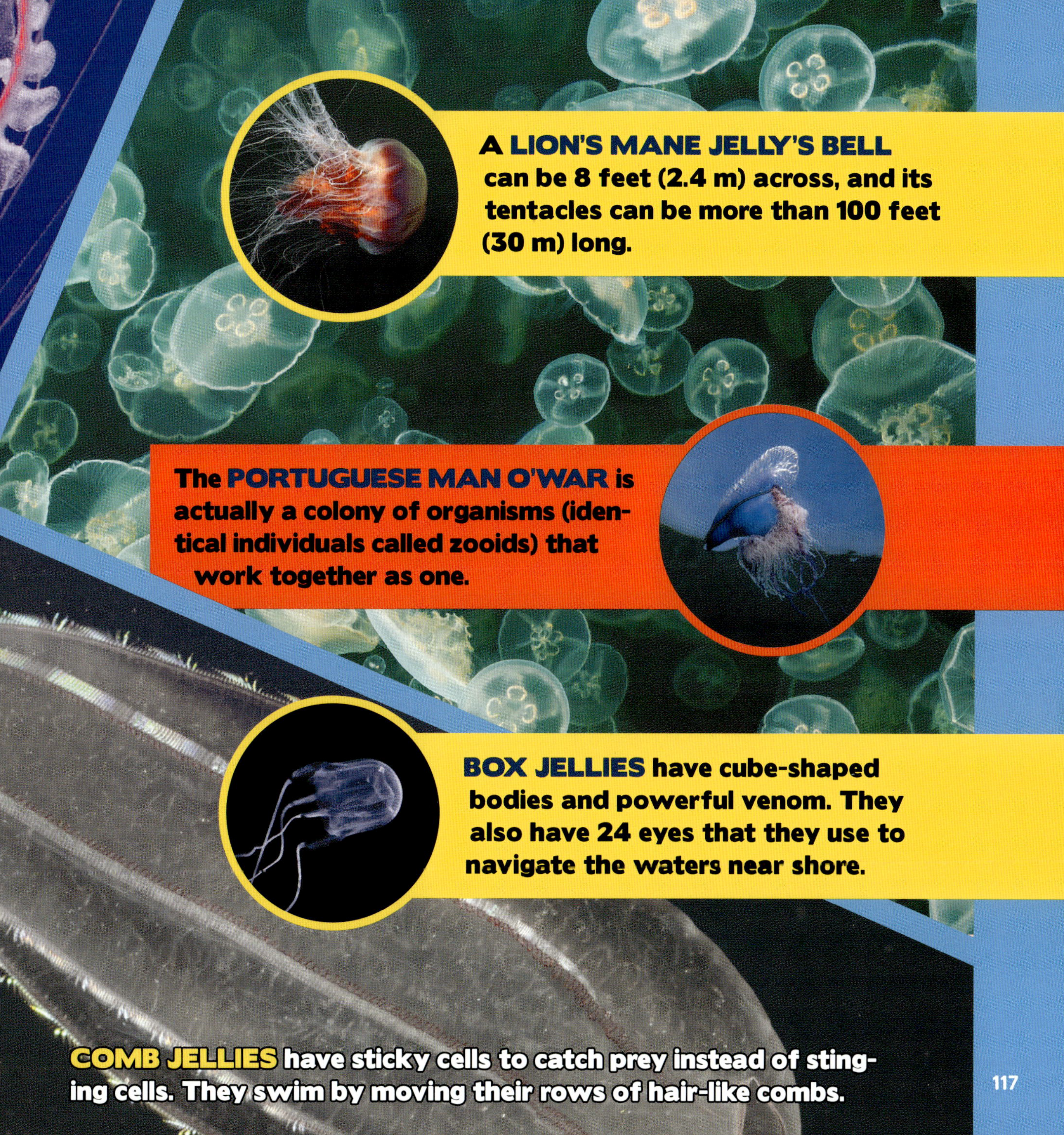

A **LION'S MANE JELLY'S BELL** can be 8 feet (2.4 m) across, and its tentacles can be more than 100 feet (30 m) long.

The **PORTUGUESE MAN O'WAR** is actually a colony of organisms (identical individuals called zooids) that work together as one.

BOX JELLIES have cube-shaped bodies and powerful venom. They also have 24 eyes that they use to navigate the waters near shore.

COMB JELLIES have sticky cells to catch prey instead of stinging cells. They swim by moving their rows of hair-like combs.

PRICKLY PERSONALITIES

ECHINODERMS are a group of invertebrates that have hard, spiny "skin." Sea stars, sea cucumbers, sea urchins, and sand dollars are all echinoderms.

Echinoderms' bodies form a pattern around a central point, kind of like a pie cut into pieces.

SEA STARS are sometimes called "starfish," but they're not fish. They're echinoderms!

To eat, a sea star pushes its stomach out through its mouth and digests its prey outside of its body.

SEA CUCUMBERS breathe through their butts! Instead of lungs, they have respiratory trees that pull oxygen from the water they suck in through their backsides.

The **TIGER TAIL SEA CUCUMBER** can grow to be up to 6 feet long (1.8 m).

SEA URCHINS have a strong, beak-like mouth called Aristotle's lantern. They use it to eat by scraping algae off rocks.

SAND DOLLARS are flat, round, purplish animals covered by tiny spines and hairs called cilia. They use these spines to move food to their mouths.

REEF LIFE

CORAL REEFS are colorful, vibrant ecosystems often found near coasts in warm, tropical waters. They cover just 2 percent of the seafloor.

At least 25 percent of marine life relies on coral reefs at some point in their lives for food, shelter, or a place to raise babies.

Coral reefs aren't rocks. REEF-BUILDING CORALS are invertebrates with soft bodies that build stony exoskeletons around themselves. Together, these exoskeletons make up a coral reef.

Like trees, some corals' exoskeletons have annual GROWTH RINGS. Scientists can use these growth rings to figure out how old a reef is.

At night, animals like chambered nautiluses come up to coral reefs to hunt. Zooplankton migrate to reefs from deeper waters to eat phytoplankton.

Not all corals form reefs. Instead of producing stony exoskeletons, many "soft" corals have tiny spikes called **SCLERITES**, which help protect their soft bodies.

Most reef-building corals grow less than 1 inch (2.5 cm) per year! It can take **THOUSANDS OF YEARS** for a coral reef to form.

Corals extend their **STINGING TENTACLES** at night to capture and eat zooplankton.

SEAHORSES AND SEA DRAGONS

PYGMY SEAHORSES are tiny—usually just 0.5 inches (1.3 cm) to 1 inch (2.5 cm) long. Their bodies match their gorgonian coral homes perfectly.

Since seahorses aren't good swimmers, they wrap their tails around corals and seagrasses to keep from being pushed around by waves.

SEA DRAGONS are seahorse relatives that live in coastal waters surrounding Australia. There are three known species: weedy sea dragons, leafy sea dragons, and ruby sea dragons.

Seahorses and sea dragons have **LONG SNOUTS AND NO TEETH**. They suck food straight into their mouths!

MALE SEAHORSES and **MALE SEA DRAGONS** give birth to babies instead of the females.

Scientists discovered a new species of sea dragon in 2015—**THE RUBY SEA DRAGON**!

LEAFY SEA DRAGONS' camouflage is so effective, these animals have no known natural predators.

THE GREAT BARRIER REEF

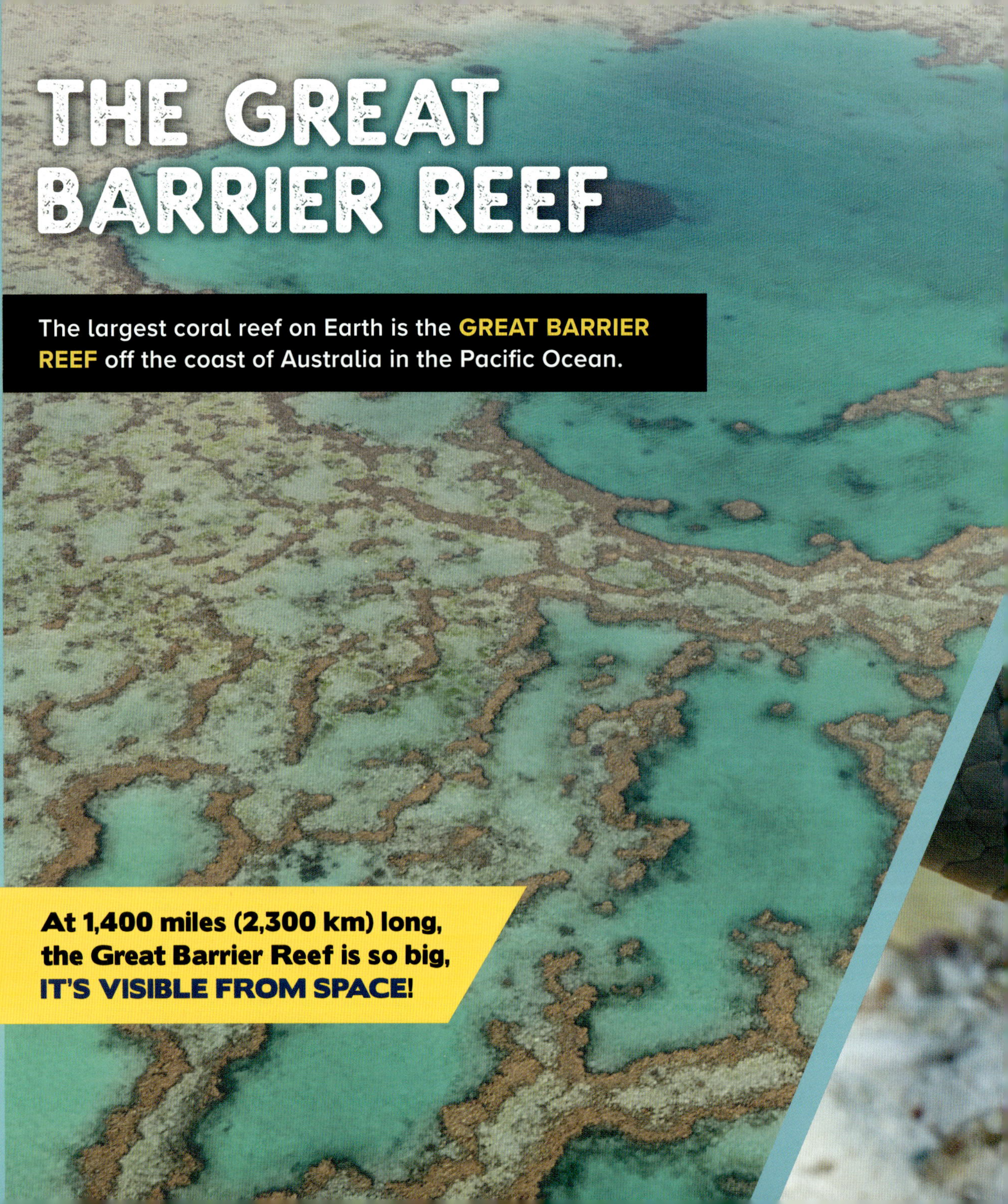

The largest coral reef on Earth is the **GREAT BARRIER REEF** off the coast of Australia in the Pacific Ocean.

At 1,400 miles (2,300 km) long, the Great Barrier Reef is so big, IT'S VISIBLE FROM SPACE!

The Great Barrier Reef is home to thousands of species, including about 400 coral species, 6 of the 7 sea turtle species, and more than 1,500 fish species.

More than a dozen species of **SEA SNAKE** live on the Great Barrier Reef. The olive sea snake is dangerously venomous—capable of killing a human with its bite, though unlikely to do so.

REEF RELATIONSHIPS

In biology, a **SYMBIOTIC RELATIONSHIP** is a relationship between two species that benefits at least one of the species.

Types of symbiotic relationships include MUTUALISM (both species benefit), COMMENSALISM (one species benefits), and PARASITISM (one species benefits by harming the other).

CLOWNFISHES live safely among the stinging tentacles of SEA ANEMONES. The sea anemone protects the clownfish, and the clownfish's poop helps nourish the anemone.

Reef fishes like sharks and eels line up to have their bodies (even their mouths) cleaned by cleaner wrasses or shrimps. These areas are called **CLEANING STATIONS**.

Algae called **ZOOXANTHELLAE** live inside **REEF-BUILDING CORALS' BODIES**. The algae create energy for the coral through photosynthesis. The corals provide a home for the algae.

The **CLEANER SHRIMP** waves its antennae to let reef fishes know when it's available to provide cleaning services.

REMORA FISHES attach themselves to **SHARKS** with their suction-cup mouths and ride them around, eating the sharks' leftovers. In exchange, remoras clean parasites off the sharks' skin.

PEARLFISHES sometimes live in **SEA CUCUMBERS**' backsides. The pearlfish backs in with its head poking out, and then pulls itself in completely to hide from predators.

COOL DEFENSES

A sea anemone's tentacles are covered in **NEMATOCYSTS**—stinging cells that inject venom into whatever they touch.

When threatened, PUFFERFISHES can double or even triple in size by swallowing water or air. Most puffers are poison-ous, but sharks seem to be immune to puffers' poison.

Don't mess with a REEF STONEFISH! It has 13 needle-like spines that can inject deadly venom into its attacker.

SEA CUCUMBERS can eject some of their organs if they need to defend themselves. They regrow the lost organs within a few weeks.

To escape a hungry predator, a **SEA STAR** can let go of an arm and regrow it later.

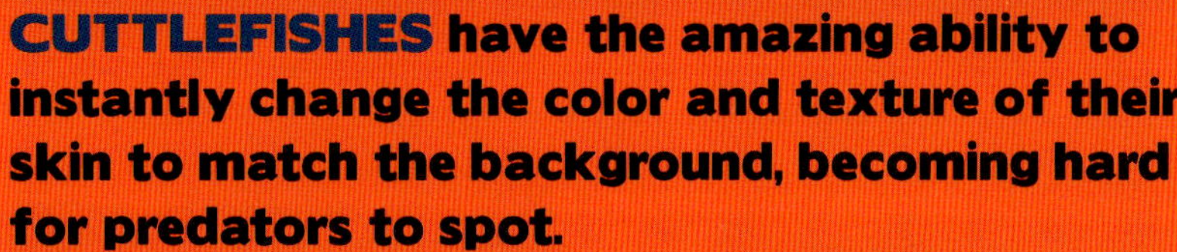

CUTTLEFISHES have the amazing ability to instantly change the color and texture of their skin to match the background, becoming hard for predators to spot.

Sea slugs called **NUDIBRANCHS** often have bright colors and bold patterns to warn predators to stay away.

ELECTRIC RAYS often live in shallow water near coral or rocky reefs. These animals stun predators and prey by giving them a strong electric shock.

BIVALVES: BETTER TOGETHER!

BIVALVES are animals that have a two-part shell connected by a hinge—like oysters, clams, mussels, and scallops.

GIANT CLAMS can weigh more than 500 pounds (227 kg)! Photosynthetic algae live in giant clams' tissues, giving the clams energy and a colorful appearance.

OYSTERS make pearls to protect themselves. They cover irritating things like bits of sand with layers of a mineral substance called nacre, eventually forming pearls.

KELP FORESTS

KELP are giant algae that can grow more than 100 feet (30 m) up from the seafloor. They grow fast—up to 2 feet (0.6 m) per day!

Instead of roots, kelp have HOLDFASTS that attach to the rocky seafloor. Animals like sea urchins and brittle stars eat the holdfasts.

KELP FORESTS grow near rocky coastlines in cool, nutrient-rich, sunlit water. Many fishes, marine mammals, and invertebrates rely on these underwater forests for food and shelter.

GAS-FILLED BLADDERS are like tiny balloons that help kelp blades stay afloat. They keep the kelp blades close to the surface so they can absorb sunlight for photosynthesis.

FOREST FRIENDS

Sea otters help keep kelp forests healthy by eating sea urchins, which can destroy a kelp forest if left unchecked.

The CALIFORNIA SHEEPHEAD grinds sea urchins and other hard-shelled prey in its throat. At night, it covers itself in mucus so predators can't smell it.

When **SEA OTTERS** need to rest while foraging in the kelp forest, they wrap kelp blades around themselves so they stay put.

The **KELP SNAIL** crawls up the kelp during the day, eats some of it, and then crawls back down at night.

GRAY WHALE MOMS sometimes lead their calves through kelp forests, possibly to avoid predators like orcas.

MEADOWS UNDER THE SEA

There are more than 70 species of **SEAGRASSES**, including eelgrass and turtle grass.

In shallow coastal areas, seagrasses can form UNDERWATER MEADOWS that provide animals with food, shelter, and protection from predators. Many fishes live there while they're young.

SEAGRASS BEDS benefit humans by reducing the impact of storms on coastlines, improving water quality, and producing oxygen through photosynthesis.

Many herbivores graze on seagrasses, including sea turtles, manatees, and geese. A green sea turtle can eat more than 4 pounds (1.8 kg) of seagrass a day!

MARINE REPTILES

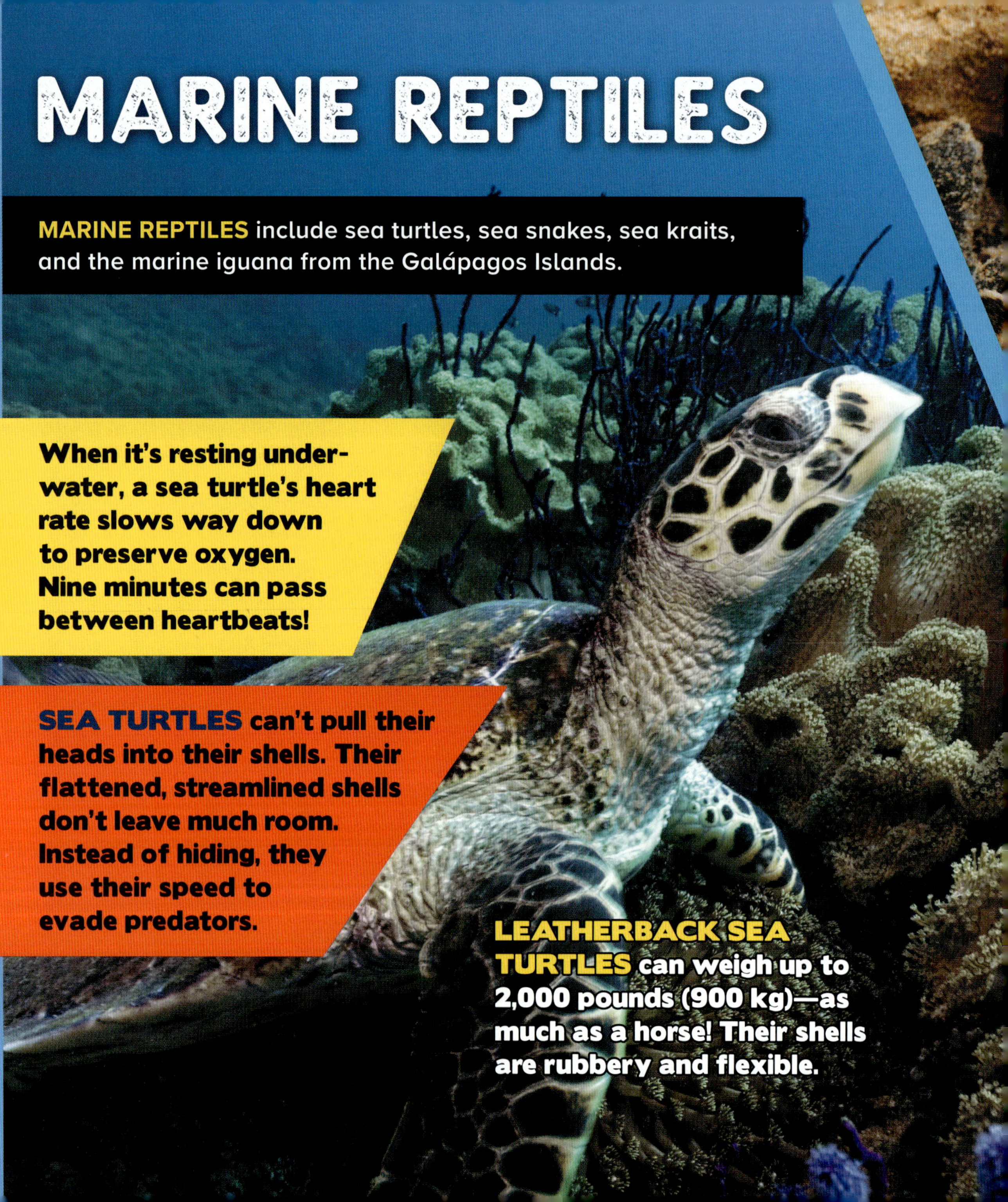

MARINE REPTILES include sea turtles, sea snakes, sea kraits, and the marine iguana from the Galápagos Islands.

When it's resting underwater, a sea turtle's heart rate slows way down to preserve oxygen. Nine minutes can pass between heartbeats!

SEA TURTLES can't pull their heads into their shells. Their flattened, streamlined shells don't leave much room. Instead of hiding, they use their speed to evade predators.

LEATHERBACK SEA TURTLES can weigh up to 2,000 pounds (900 kg)—as much as a horse! Their shells are rubbery and flexible.

Temperature determines whether sea turtle eggs develop as female or male. Females hatch from warmer nests, and males hatch from cooler nests.

MARINE IGUANAS can shrink their bodies by 20 percent when food is scarce and then return to normal size once food is abundant again.

Some sea snakes live their entire lives in the ocean, while others (called sea kraits) live part-time on land and part-time in the water.

All **SEA SNAKES** are venomous (capable of injecting venom) and can breathe through their skin.

MANGROVES: TREES ON STILTS!

MANGROVE TREES can grow in salty water. To get rid of extra salt, some mangroves "sweat" salt through their leaves.

Many mangrove tree species have above-ground roots called "PROP ROOTS." The trees appear to be standing on top of their roots like stilts!

MANGROVE ROOTS trap dirt, creating a muddy bottom where animals like horseshoe crabs live. The roots also serve as nurseries for fishes, crustaceans, and shellfishes.

A very unique predator roams the Sundarbans mangrove swamps of Bangladesh and India—the mighty **BENGAL TIGER**!

EXPLORING ESTUARIES

ESTUARIES form along coasts where rivers and streams run into the ocean. This mix of fresh and salt water is called brackish water.

Dragonflies and other insects, shore birds like great blue herons, false water rats, and even saltwater crocodiles live in or near estuaries around the world.

The estuarian or saltwater **CROCODILE** can be around 20 feet (6 m) long and may live up to 80 years! Australians call these crocs "salties."

DEEP

MORE THAN 80 PERCENT OF THE OCEAN HAS YET TO BE EXPLORED.

ROCK BOTTOM

People living before the 19th century generally believed the **SEAFLOOR** was flat and empty.

The bottom of the ocean has underwater canyons, trenches, mountains, volcanoes, and plenty of life. It's also constantly changing.

Earth's surface is split into seven large TECTONIC PLATES, plus some smaller plates. These plates move, shift, spread, and collide, sometimes causing earthquakes and tsunamis.

Underwater volcanic eruptions occur at MID-OCEAN RIDGES—places where tectonic plates move away from each other. These eruptions create new oceanic crust.

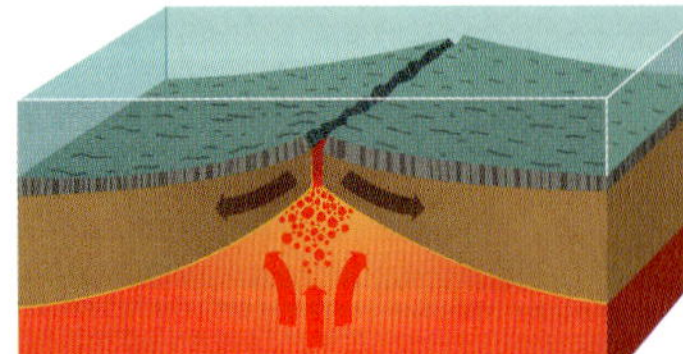

The longest mountain range on Earth, the **MID-OCEAN RIDGE SYSTEM**, is at the bottom of the ocean. It's a long chain of volcanoes that stretches for 40,000 miles (64,370 km).

Mid-ocean ridges spread at different rates. Each year, the Mid-Atlantic Ridge spreads up to 2 inches (5 cm), while the East Pacific Rise spreads up to 6 inches (15 cm).

Even at 29,032 feet (8,849 m), Mount Everest isn't Earth's tallest mountain. Hawaii's **MAUNA KEA** is 33,500 feet (10,210 m) tall, but more than half of it is underwater.

The Hawaiian islands were formed by a **VOLCANIC HOTSPOT** in the Pacific Ocean. A new island is being formed right now by an underwater volcano called Lōʻihi!

IN THE TRENCHES

HUGE UNDERWATER TRENCHES form in the ocean where tectonic plates are pushing together—forcing one plate to slide beneath the other.

Earth's longest ocean trench is the **PERU-CHILE TRENCH** in the Pacific. It's about 3,700 miles (6,000 km) long and 40 miles (64 km) wide, on average.

The **MARIANA TRENCH** is near Guam, a U.S. territory in the Pacific Ocean. Much of the trench is protected as a U.S. national monument.

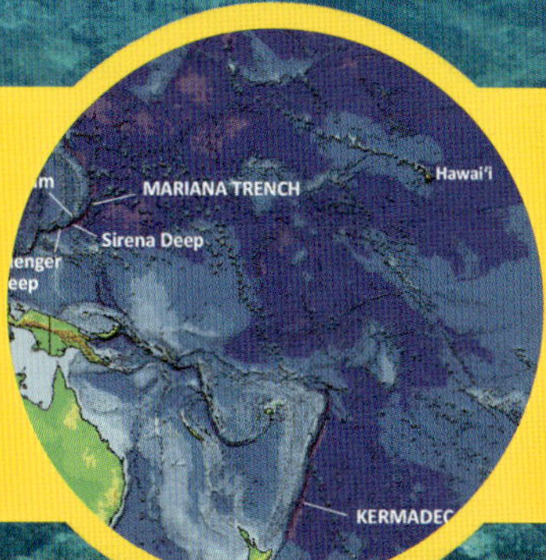

The deepest place on Earth is inside the Mariana Trench in the Pacific Ocean. It's called **CHALLENGER DEEP**, and it's almost 7 miles (11.3 km) below the surface.

The Mariana Trench's depth was first measured by the **CHALLENGER EXPEDITION** in 1875. They measured it by lowering a weighted line down until it hit the bottom.

THE CHALLENGER DEEP

The first people to explore the Challenger Deep were **JACQUES PICCARD** and **DON WALSH** aboard a submersible called the *Trieste* in 1960.

To date, the only other person who's visited the Challenger Deep is JAMES CAMERON—a filmmaker—who dove solo in the *Deepsea Challenger* in 2012.

Even the deepest place in the world isn't quiet. Scientists recorded NOISES in the Challenger Deep and detected earthquakes, moaning whales, and even ship propellers.

DEEP-SEA LIFE

There's **NO SUNLIGHT** in the deep sea. In general, it's dark and very cold, with an average temperature of 39°F (3.9°C).

The pressure just 3 miles (4.8 km) down under the water is more than 500 times what it is at the surface.

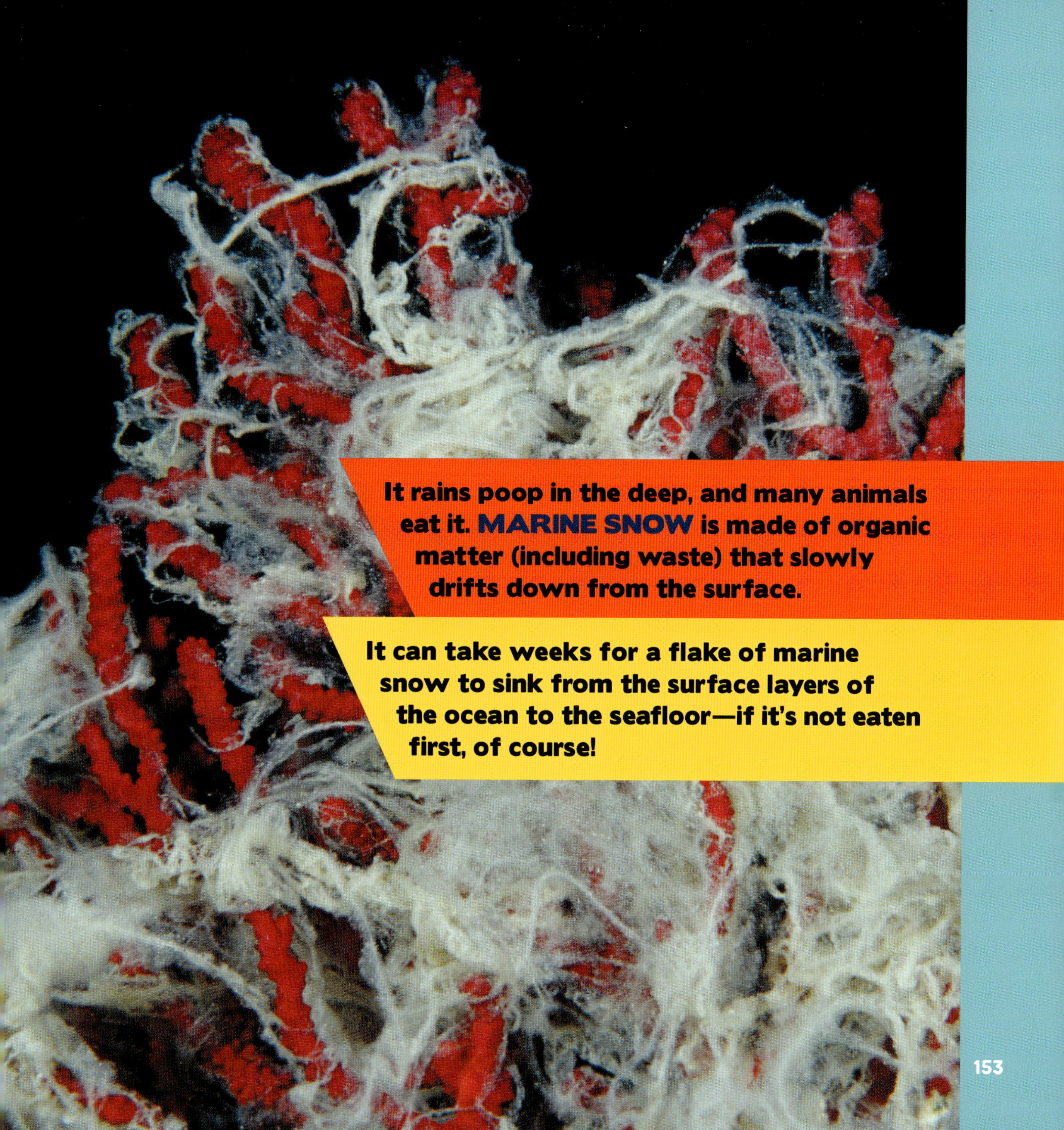

It rains poop in the deep, and many animals eat it. **MARINE SNOW** is made of organic matter (including waste) that slowly drifts down from the surface.

It can take weeks for a flake of marine snow to sink from the surface layers of the ocean to the seafloor—if it's not eaten first, of course!

TRICKS FOR LIVING IN THE DARK

Many deep-sea animals are **BIOLUMINESCENT** and create their own light! Bioluminescence helps animals hunt, defend themselves, and communicate with both friends and foes.

A deep-sea worm called the GREEN BOMBER distracts predators by releasing fluid-filled, balloon-like structures that burst into light and then fade seconds later.

Deep-sea fishes called BARRELEYES have tube-shaped eyes and dome-like, see-through heads. They rotate their eyes up to search for prey directly above them.

Some animals, like lanternfishes, have special organs called **PHOTOPHORES** that produce light. Others, like anglerfishes, light up thanks to the **BIOLUMINESCENT BACTERIA** in their bodies.

The female **DEEP-SEA ANGLERFISH** has a fleshy "lure" on top of her head that can light up to attract prey. When dinner gets close, she strikes!

Some animals in the deep sea, like **VIPERFISH**, have large eyes to let in as much light as possible.

OCTOPUSES VS. SQUIDS

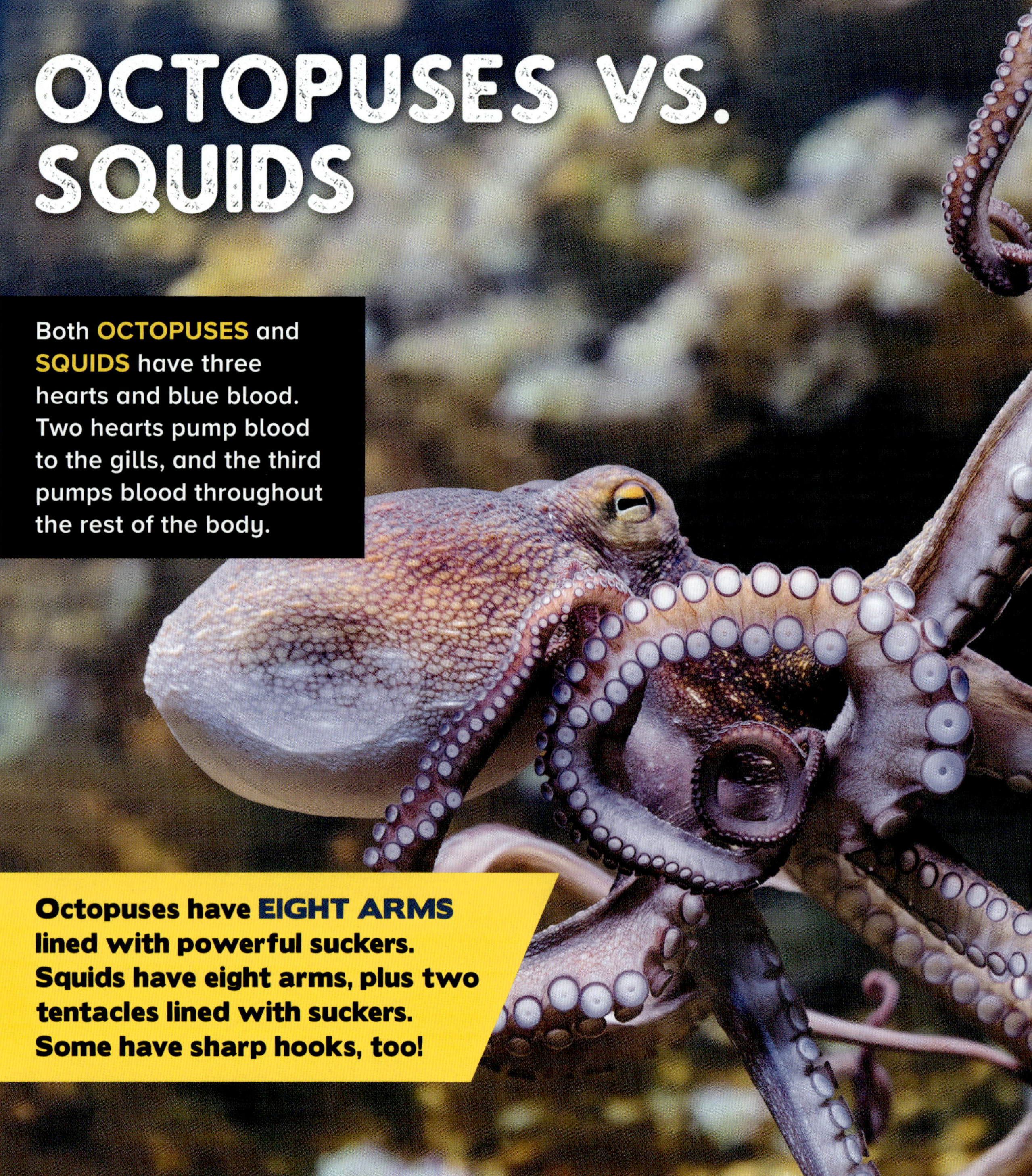

Both **OCTOPUSES** and **SQUIDS** have three hearts and blue blood. Two hearts pump blood to the gills, and the third pumps blood throughout the rest of the body.

Octopuses have EIGHT ARMS lined with powerful suckers. Squids have eight arms, plus two tentacles lined with suckers. Some have sharp hooks, too!

Squid and octopus bodies are soft except for their beaks. These animals' tough beaks—along with a tongue-like structure called a radula—help them eat hard-shelled prey.

In place of suckers, the **GLOWING SUCKER OCTOPUS** has organs capable of flashing light. Scientists believe this may help the octopus attract prey.

Many squids and octopuses release a cloud of **DARK INK** to distract predators. Deep-sea species like the vampire squid release **BIOLUMINESCENT MUCUS** instead.

SUPER-SIZED SQUIDS

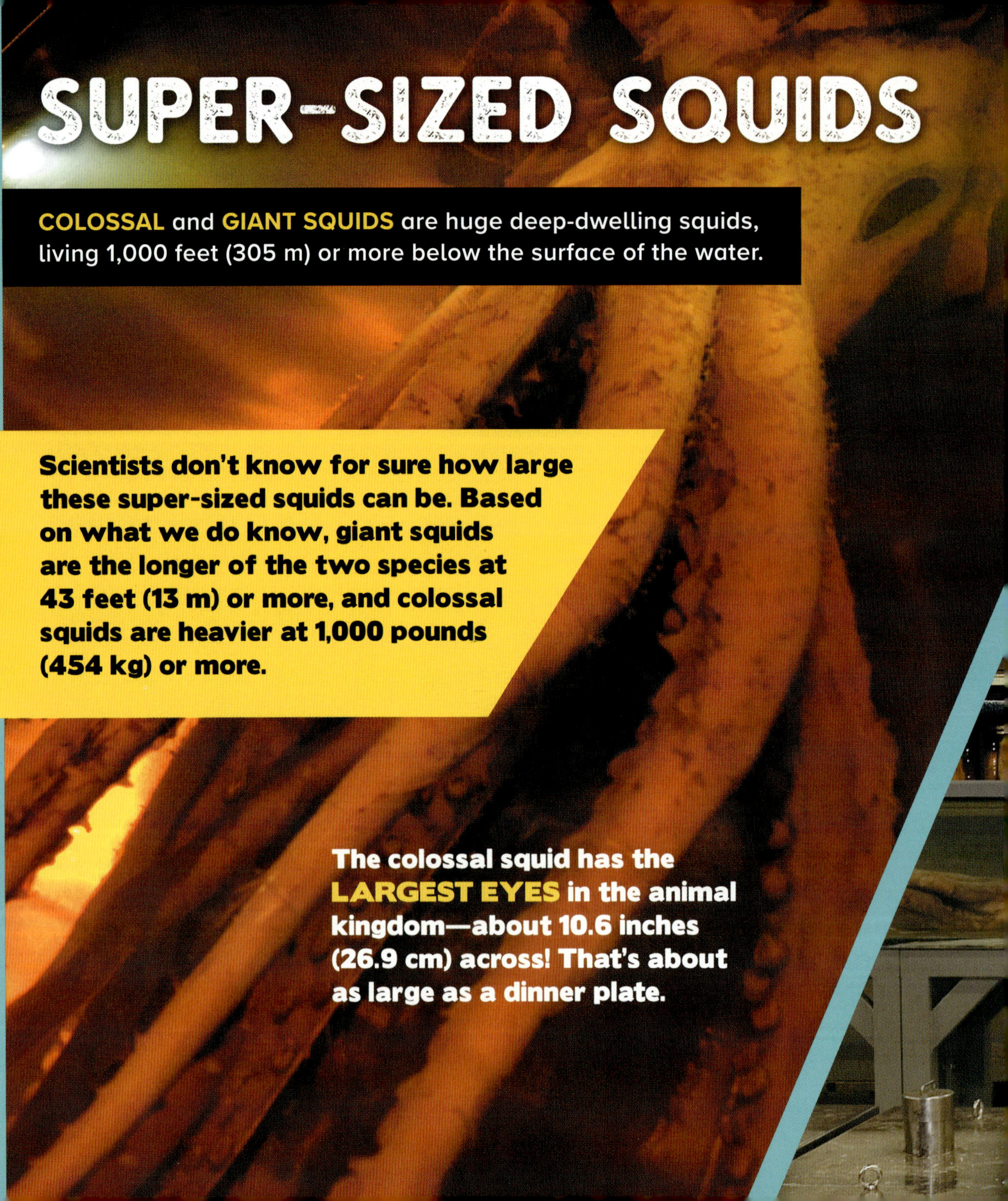

COLOSSAL and **GIANT SQUIDS** are huge deep-dwelling squids, living 1,000 feet (305 m) or more below the surface of the water.

Scientists don't know for sure how large these super-sized squids can be. Based on what we do know, giant squids are the longer of the two species at 43 feet (13 m) or more, and colossal squids are heavier at 1,000 pounds (454 kg) or more.

The colossal squid has the LARGEST EYES in the animal kingdom—about 10.6 inches (26.9 cm) across! That's about as large as a dinner plate.

These large squids' only predator is the **DEEP-DIVING SPERM WHALE.** When sperm whales die, scientists find giant and colossal squid beaks inside their stomachs.

A COLOSSAL SQUID, frozen for science in 2007, took 60 hours to thaw. The defrosted "squidcicle" is now on display at New Zealand's Te Papa Tongarewa Museum.

WARMTH IN COLD PLACES

HYDROTHERMAL VENTS spew superhot water (up to 750°F/398°C) out of cracks in the seafloor. These vents support entire communities of life in the deep.

Hydrothermal vents called BLACK SMOKERS look like they're spitting out black smoke. Vents called white smokers look like they're spitting out white smoke.

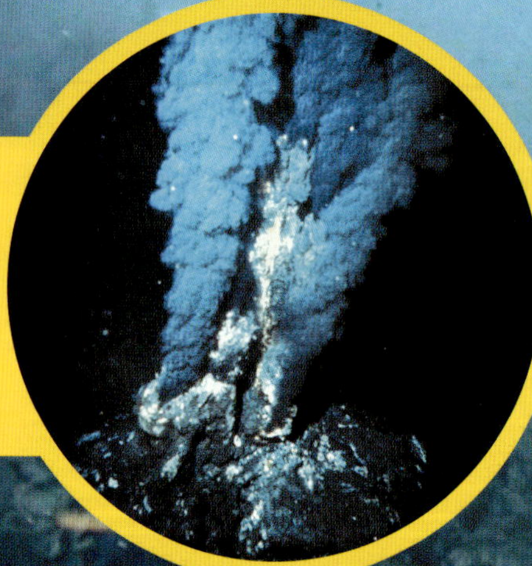

Bacteria that turn chemicals into energy through a process called **CHEMOSYNTHESIS** form the base of hydrothermal vent food chains.

GIANT TUBE WORMS, feather duster worms, vent crabs, and deep-sea mussels often live near hydrothermal vents.

DEEP-SEA COMMUNITIES

COLD SEEPS occur where chemicals leak out of cracks in the seafloor. Bacteria mats form near these seeps and attract animals like worms, shrimps, and snails.

There are "lakes" called BRINE POOLS on the seafloor. Some organisms thrive along the edges of these lakes, which contain saltier-than-usual seawater.

Deep-sea communities form around **WHALE CARCASSES** that sink to the seafloor. Ratfishes, squat lobsters, sleeper sharks, worms, and bacteria feast on a single whale carcass for years.

Bone-eating osedax worms, nicknamed "**ZOMBIE WORMS**," dissolve the bones of whale carcasses that have fallen to the seafloor.

SHIPWRECKS

After ships sink, they often become ecosystems. A wreck may be home to corals, anemones, barnacles, sharks, and schools of fishes.

There may be as many as 3 million SHIPWRECKS scattered across the ocean floor.

In 2011, marine archaeologists found a shipwreck off the coast of Japan. It is believed to be part of KUBLAI KHAN'S LOST FLEET, which sank more than 700 years ago.

In 2019, researchers found THE DEEPEST SHIPWRECK discovered to date—a World War II destroyer ship that lies 20,400 feet (6,218 m) beneath the surface.

Real-life treasure hunters found about 14 tons (12.7 tonnes) of gold, silver, and other treasure on a sunken Spanish vessel in 2007.

A German ocean liner called the **MV WILHELM GUSTLOFF** sank in 1945 and took 9,000 passengers with it. It is the deadliest known shipwreck in history.

Christopher Columbus set out to discover the New World with three ships in 1492. One ship, the **SANTA MARIA**, sank during the journey and still hasn't been found.

Ships aren't the only vessels littering the seafloor. **SUBMARINES** and even **PLANES** have found their way to the bottom of the ocean.

THE UNSINKABLE SHIP

The "unsinkable" **RMS *TITANIC*** sank in 1912 after striking an iceberg. About 700 people survived, but more than 1,500 people died.

Oceanographer ROBERT BALLARD was conducting secret research for the U.S. Navy when he and his crew discovered the *Titanic* wreck in 1985—13,000 feet (4,000 m) below the surface.

A 2010 expedition used underwater robots to document the *Titanic*'s "**DEBRIS FIELD**"—a 3-by-5-mile (4.8-by-8 km) section of seafloor filled with wreckage from the ship.

Seven decades after *Titanic*'s discovery, researchers hauled many items to the surface: clothes, dishes, jewelry, and even a **POCKET WATCH** that stopped when its owner fell into the sea (1:45 a.m.).

CURIOUS CREATURES OF THE DEEP

The **GOBLIN SHARK** has extendable jaws. This shark thrusts out its jaw to snatch a fish or squid, then pulls it back into its mouth.

TRIPOD FISHES perch themselves on the seafloor facing the current and wait for food like zooplankton to pass by.

The **BLOBFISH** was voted the world's ugliest animal. Its squishy body looks strange on land, but it is perfectly built to survive the pressure in the deep.

A deep-dwelling, bioluminescent siphonophore called the **GIANT SIPHONOPHORE** can be 130 feet (39 m) long—that's longer than a blue whale!

SEA PIGS are 6.5-inch-long (16-cm-long) transparent sea cucumbers that form herds on the seafloor wherever there's food—like at a whale fall.

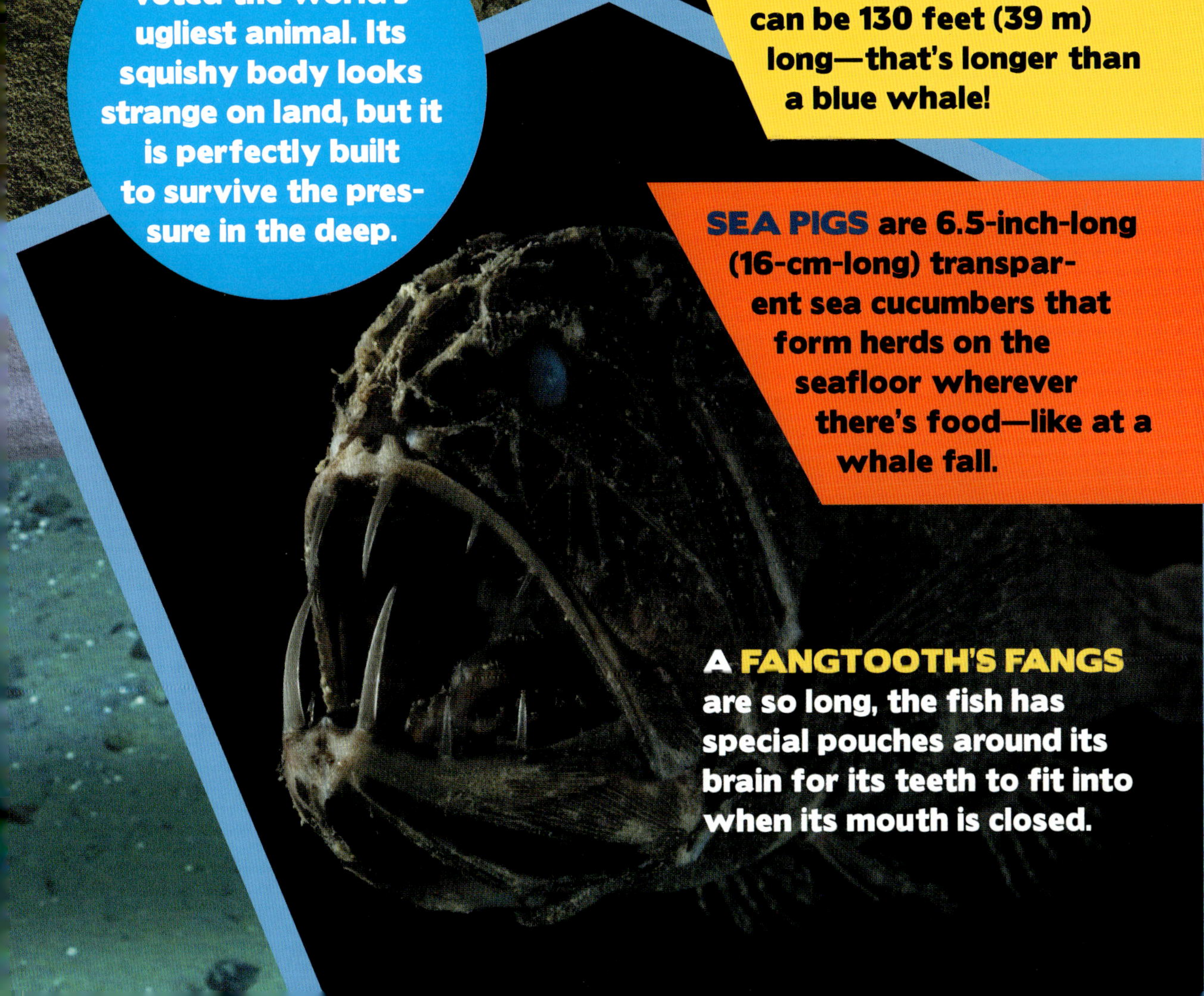

A **FANGTOOTH'S FANGS** are so long, the fish has special pouches around its brain for its teeth to fit into when its mouth is closed.

Chapter 6

POLE TO POLE

POLAR BEARS AND PENGUINS LIVE ON OPPOSITE POLES. YOU'LL NEVER SEE THEM TOGETHER IN THE WILD.

NORTH POLE, SOUTH POLE

The **NORTH POLE** is in the Arctic Ocean, and the **SOUTH POLE** is in Antarctica, an ice-covered continent in the Southern Ocean.

POLARIS, or the North Star, shines in the sky just above the North Pole and does not move. Civilizations have used this star for navigation for centuries.

At each pole, there's up to 24 hours of sunlight on summer days and up to 24 hours of darkness on winter days.

Each New Year's Day, scientists at the **AMUNDSEN-SCOTT SOUTH POLE STATION** put up a ceremonial pole at Earth's southernmost point, which shifts each year.

The South Pole is colder than the North Pole. Average winter temperatures are -40°F (-42°C) at the North Pole and -76°F (-60°C) at the South Pole.

GLORIOUS GLACIERS

A **GLACIER** forms when snow piles up year after year and compresses into thick, solid ice. Glaciers cover about 10 percent of the land on Earth.

Glaciers don't stay in one place—they move. Gravity causes most glaciers to move slowly, just an inch (25 mm) or so per day, but some move faster.

Some glaciers form high up in mountains and flow down into valleys. Glaciers called ICE CAPS form on flat ground and move in all directions.

The JAKOBSHAVN GLACIER IN GREENLAND broke a glacial speed record in 2014 when scientists observed it moving at a rate of 150 feet (45.7 m) per day.

ICE SHEETS (large ice caps) cover Greenland in the Arctic and the continent of Antarctica. Together, these two ice sheets contain 99 percent of Earth's freshwater ice.

FLOATING ICE MOUNTAINS

When a huge chunk of ice breaks off a glacier, an iceberg is born. This is called **CALVING**.

The ICEBERG you can see is only a tiny piece of the whole thing. Almost 90 percent of an ice-berg is underwater.

A broken-off piece of the **JAKOBSHAVN GLACIER** may have been what sunk the *Titanic.*

An iceberg smaller than about 6.5 feet (1.98 m) across is called a "**GROWLER.**"

WELCOME TO THE ARCTIC

Eight countries border the Arctic Ocean: Canada, Finland, Greenland, Iceland, Norway, Russia, Sweden, and the United States (Alaska).

ARCTIC SEA ICE is constantly changing—growing and shrinking depending on the season. It never completely melts, even in the summer.

Unlike glaciers and icebergs, which are made of frozen freshwater, sea ice is made of **FROZEN SALT WATER.**

Most **ARCTIC SEA ICE** is 6 to 9 feet (1.8 to 2.7 m) thick, but it can be up to 15 feet (4.5 m) thick in some places!

Sea ice reflects 80 percent of sunlight beaming down on it, which helps keep the Arctic cold.

NORTH POLE RESIDENTS

Several seal species and walruses live year-round in the Arctic. They rest and give birth on the sea ice.

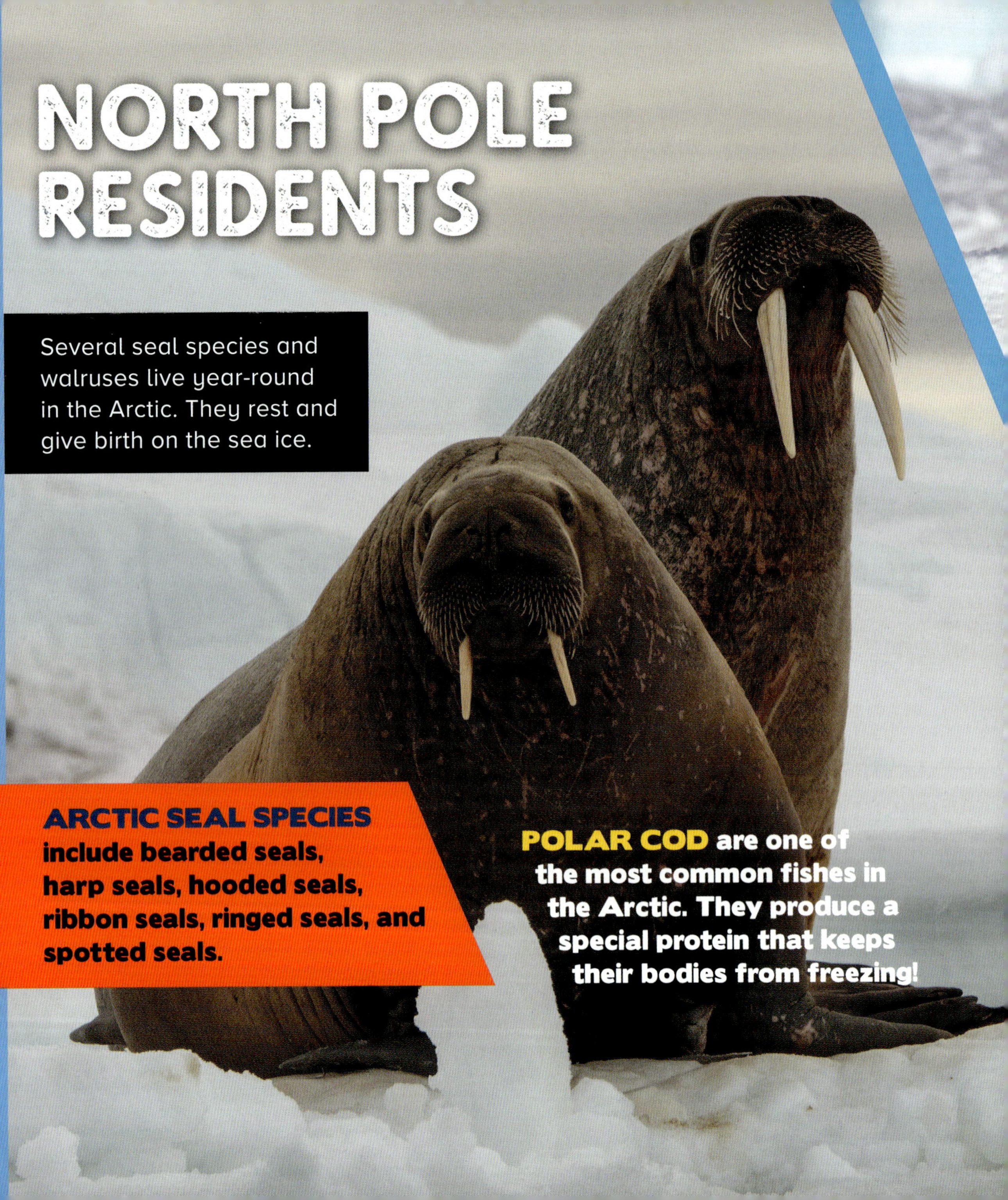

ARCTIC SEAL SPECIES include bearded seals, harp seals, hooded seals, ribbon seals, ringed seals, and spotted seals.

POLAR COD are one of the most common fishes in the Arctic. They produce a special protein that keeps their bodies from freezing!

Some marine mammals, like belugas, narwhals, and bowhead whales, live year-round in the Arctic. Others, like gray and humpback whales, visit each summer.

ICE ALGAE live inside and under sea ice. Krill and other zooplankton eat the ice algae.

THE ULTIMATE POLE PREDATOR

POLAR BEARS are the top Arctic predators. They hunt seals by waiting for them to pop out of breathing holes in the sea ice.

A polar bear's skin is black, and its fur isn't actually white. Each hair is hollow and see-through, but it looks white because it reflects light.

Polar bears can have up to 4.5 inches (11.4 cm) of fat to help keep their bodies warm.

A polar bear doesn't slip when it walks on ice because it has GRIPPY FOOTPADS covered with small bumps called papillae.

BEAUTIFUL BELUGAS

BELUGAS don't have a dorsal (back) fin. It's a good thing they don't, since they swim just beneath the sea ice looking for breathing holes.

BABY BELUGAS (called calves) are born gray and turn white as they get older. Adult belugas' white color blends in with their icy habitat.

Unlike most whales, belugas can turn their heads up, down, and side to side.

Belugas use their **BLOWHOLES** to make many different sounds that help them communicate with each other, including a chirping noise that sounds like a bird.

UNICORNS OF THE SEA

Unlike other toothed whales, the **NARWHAL** doesn't have teeth in its mouth. Instead, it has a long, spiraled tusk (which is actually a tooth!) that grows through its upper lip.

NARWHAL TUSKS can be about 10 feet (3 m) long and are covered with millions of nerve endings, making them very sensitive.

Since male narwhals have tusks more often than females (who rarely grow them), scientists think the tusks' purpose may be to impress females.

Narwhals are **PICKY EATERS**. During winter, they gorge mostly on Greenland halibut and Gonatus squid. In summer, they don't eat much at all.

ARCTIC SEABIRDS

Because seabirds drink salty seawater, they have **GLANDS** near their eyes to help them get rid of the extra salt in their bodies.

ATLANTIC PUFFIN COUPLES often reunite each breeding season, sometimes at the same nest burrow. They tap their bills together to strengthen their bond.

ARCTIC TERNS migrate from pole to pole every year. Over its lifetime, an Arctic tern travels a distance equivalent to three trips to the moon and back.

A **BLACK GUILLEMOT** is only black during the summer breeding season. In winter, it is mostly white.

WELCOME TO THE ANTARCTIC

ANTARCTICA is the fifth largest continent on Earth, and it's almost entirely covered by an ice sheet.

Antarctica is so dry it's technically a DESERT—a very cold desert!

The SOUTHERN OCEAN'S boundaries aren't official. In fact, not all scientists agree that the Southern Ocean is a separate ocean basin at all.

The COLDEST RECORDED TEMPERATURE ON EARTH was measured in Antarctica in 1983: -128.6°F (-89.2°C)!

HOME, CHILLY HOME

ANTARCTIC ICEFISHES have colorless blood. Their blood doesn't have red blood cells, so it's thinner and requires less energy to transport oxygen throughout the icefishes' bodies.

ANTARCTIC KRILL swarm in huge numbers. In 2019, an Australian research vessel measured a swarm that was about 1,300 feet (396 m) long and 325 feet (99 m) deep.

CRABEATER SEALS don't eat crabs. They have unique teeth that allow them to strain their food, mostly Antarctic krill, from the water.

Weddell seals, Ross seals, leopard seals, crabeater seals, Antarctic fur seals, and southern elephant seals all call Antarctica home.

SEVERAL WHALE SPECIES spend summers feeding in Antarctica, including blue whales, sei whales, minke whales, humpback whales, fin whales, southern right whales, and orcas.

LEOPARD SEALS and **ORCAS** are top predators in the Antarctic. Both hunt seals and penguins.

No one knows how big the crabeater seal population is, but it could be up to 15 million. They may be the world's most numerous large mammal.

SEABIRDS OF THE ANTARCTIC

WANDERING ALBATROSSES have the largest wingspan of any bird—up to 11 feet (3.3 m)! That's about as wide as a small car is long.

ALBATROSSES are birds of legend. Some people believe these majestic sea-birds carry the souls of sailors lost at sea.

ANTARCTIC PRIONS strain zooplankton out of the Southern Ocean with their specialized beaks—similar to how baleen whales feed.

PETRELS take off for flight by "running" on the surface of the water.

PENGUINS

Penguins can't fly, but they are **EXPERT SWIMMERS**. Their wings, which are like flippers, are perfect for swimming and diving in the ocean.

PENGUINS move on land by wad-dling, hopping, and even sliding on their bellies.

EMPEROR PENGUINS are the largest pen-guins on Earth. They can be 4 feet (1.3 m) tall!

The emperor penguin dad is in charge of hatch-ing the egg. He balances his egg on his feet and covers it with his warm feathers. He doesn't eat until the egg hatches.

Penguins sometimes eat **SNOW** when they are thirsty. They may also eat snow to cool off if they get too warm.

There are millions of **ADÉLIE PENGUINS** in Antarctica! These little penguins don't like to be the first one in the water. Once one member of the group safely dives in, the rest follow.

ROCKHOPPER PENGUINS have red eyes and spiky yellow feathers on their heads.

Not all penguins live in cold weather. Galápagos penguins, African penguins, and Magellanic penguins live in **WARM CLIMATES**.

POLAR EXPLORATION

British explorer **JOHN FRANKLIN** and crew vanished in 1845 while attempting to sail to the North Pole. Franklin's sunken ship was found in 2014—169 years later!

Americans FREDERICK COOK and ROBERT PEARY each claimed to have been the first to reach the North Pole—Cook in 1908 and Peary in 1909.

Peary often gets credit for discovering the North Pole, but evidence suggests he and his team may not have actually reached it. It remains a mystery.

The first explorers to reach the South Pole were Norwegian **ROALD AMUNDSEN** and his team. They arrived on December 14, 1911.

Amundsen had planned to discover the North Pole, but when he heard Peary had reached it first, he set his sights on the South Pole instead.

ERNEST SHACKLETON and his crew survived being stranded in the Antarctic for more than a year after their ship became trapped in ice during an expedition that began in 1914.

POLES IN TROUBLE

WARMING GLOBAL TEMPERATURES are gradually melting sea ice in the Arctic and Southern Oceans.

In September 2020, summer sea ice in the Arctic was the second smallest on record. Some scientists think the Arctic's late-summer sea ice could be gone by 2040.

With less sea ice, **EARTH'S CLIMATE** will continue to change, impacting all of the animals that depend on the ocean—including humans.

It's not too late! Humans can work together to reduce our impact on Earth's climate and **PROTECT THE OCEANS**.

About the Authors

Bethanie and Josh Hestermann are authors of animal-science books for kids. They've written *Zoology for Kids: Understanding and Working with Animals*; *Marine Science for Kids: Exploring and Protecting Our Watery World*; *Search the Ocean: Find the Animals*; *Search the Zoo: Find the Animals*; and *Ocean Animals for Kids: A Junior Scientist's Guide to Whales, Sharks, and Other Marine Life*. Bethanie is a freelance writer, and Josh is a zoologist working at the Orange County Zoo. They have two children.